Air Commandos

The Quiet Professionals

Air Commandos

The Quiet Professionals
Air Force Special Operations Command

By Randy Jolly

*To the men and women of the
Air Force Special Operations Command
whose hard work, diligence and sacrifice
makes a difference when it counts.*

TABLE OF CONTENTS

International Standard Book Number 0-9624862-7-2
Library of Congress Catalog Number   94-94140
©1994 by Randy Jolly
Published by: Aero Graphics Inc.
4729 Lawler Road - Garland, Texas 75042-4506
214/276/2544 FAX - 214/276/5494
Designer - Laurie Adams
Printed in Hong Kong through Bookbuilders Ltd.

30 Years Ago. . .

AC-47 "Spooky" – early gunship

Thirty years ago the U.S. military was involved in a conflict in Southeast Asia with an enemy who utilized the cover of darkness to perform 80% of its logistic support operations.

Texas Instruments developed infrared night vision technology to deny the enemy this advantage.

Early production Forward Looking Infrared (FLIR) systems enjoyed a long service life and were maintained in the U.S. inventory into the late 1980s.

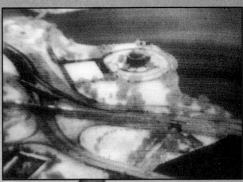

Early production FLIR imagery

Today. . .

Common Module FLIR holds an advantage over its predecessors in reliability, maintainability and reduced cost.

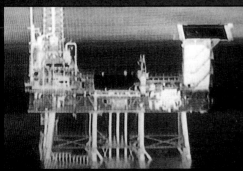

Common Module FLIR imagery

Focal Plane Array FLIR imagery

The next generation of Texas Instruments FLIR technology, the Focal Plane Array, is currently under evaluation by Special Operations units.

Texas Instruments has made bold strides in the development of Focal Plane Array FLIR systems, Local Area Processing (LAP) for enhanced image quality, Electronic Image Stabilization (EIS), and Image Fusion.

U.S. Special Operations and Texas Instruments have shared 30 years of history together. We are proud to extend this relationship into the next millennium.

TEXAS INSTRUMENTS

Defense Systems & Electronics Group

Malcolm Baldrige National Quality Award
1992 Winner

On a dark and moonless night our MH-53J Pave Low helicopter raced above the ground at tree top level. The thought going through my mind was, "If it's too dark to take photographs, why am I here?" My camera had long since been stowed, and I was hanging on for dear life witnessing in practice what Pave Low crews do for real in a "shooting war."

Only a few hours earlier I had photographed the helicopter crew as they boarded the aircraft, completed pre-flight checks, powered up the avionics, and loaded hundreds of rounds of machine gun ammunition. My task on this visit was to photograph members of the 20th Special Operations Squadron as they participated in a simulated rescue and fire support of a special forces team compromised in hostile territory. In military parlance – exfil the special forces team. In ordinary terms – rescue them from the bad guys.

Since most opportunities afforded a civilian photographer by the Air Force are on a not-to-interfere basis, my flight was to be part of a routine training mission. For the few hours of afternoon daylight remaining, I concentrated on photographs of the pilots up front as they monitored their FLIR and terrain-following/terrain-avoidance radar. I photographed the door gunners as they double checked their 7.62mm miniguns and the tail gunner as he fitted a can of .50 caliber ammunition to the pedestal mounted machine gun on the ramp at the rear of the aircraft.

In the aircraft we were all linked by voice through the intercoms in our flight helmets. The comm-cord, which was attached to each helmet and plugged into the aircraft's intercom system, and the safety harness, which was attached to the waist of the crew member and fastened to the aircraft's deck, made moving around with three other people in the back end of the Pave Low a clumsy ballet. For the uninitiated it takes very little movement to get completely tangled in the comm-cord, the safety harness, and the camera straps. This is especially true when the action to be photographed is simultaneously taking place at the gunners' stations and in the cockpit as the helicopter is bucking and sliding through low altitude turbulence.

As the mission progressed, the pilots and flight engineer methodically called out flight information (speed, altitude, and notable obstacles) while the rest of the crew reported what they saw from their perspective: how systems were operating, any air traffic, other potential problems. As I stood next to one of the gunners, we scanned the ground for high-line wires and the horizon for any traffic in our air space. The crew worked together in harmony as a well-coordinated team. Information flowed freely, back and forth, among the pilots, flight engineers, and the gunners. The big, brutish Pave Low powered on toward the pre-planned rendezvous with its "customers" – a Ranger recon team/ on the ground.

It was exhilarating to fly so fast just above the trees. The heat of the exhaust and indescribable odor of jet fuel forced by the downdraft through the open windows only emphasized the sheer power, ruggedness, and no-frills flying in the Pave Low. The deafening sound of the engines, the constant vibration, and the undulating aircraft heightened the sense of adventure, the intensity, and the danger.

As the twilight faded, so did my confidence. I had never flown in a military helicopter at night. The rigors of simulated combat heightened my anticipation and apprehension. As the darkness deepened so did my reservations about where I was and what on earth I was doing there!

As the last vestiges of light disappeared, the crew pulled their night vision goggles (NVGs) in place. Using NVGs at night is no easy task. It is like looking through a pair of small binoculars. NVGs are fitted on a mount on the forward edge of the flight helmet and brought down in front of the eyes. It is the uncanny ability to see and fly at night that gives the special operations forces one of their primary advantages.

With the aid of NVGs, the FLIR system, and the terrain-following/terrain-avoidance radar, the flying and scanning continued apace in the near total darkness. The crackle over the headsets became intense. Only specific and relevant bits of information were relayed among the crew. A gunner/scanner would call out, "Wires at ten o'clock;" or a pilot would say, "Climbing to 500," to indicate a hill or slight rise in the landscape illuminated by the FLIR. It was all business now. There was a new tension in everyone's voice. There was no small talk.

Instead of a nice little jaunt over the countryside to photograph Pave Lows in benign settings, I now found my self committed for the duration on a two-ship, nighttime training mission. This one, like all the others, was carefully planned down to the last detail. The "what if's" had been briefed, and the crew well-versed on what to do in an emergency. What if we had to land in the water? What if somebody were hurt? How would we handle it? What if a gun jammed? All the unplanned events that could endanger the mission were discussed so that everyone, even the photographer, knew his job and what to do in the event things went terribly wrong.

As the mission progressed, our two-ship formation continued to skim just above the tree tops. The sharply defined landscape as viewed through NVGs whisked by in an eerie green blur. Details were easy to see: a copse of trees to the left, a valley to the right, a narrow winding country road running at a right angle to our flight path. Without the NVGs the horizon was invisible. Sky and earth were one and the same.

A clearing measuring about a hundred yards by roughly a half mile suddenly loomed up

ahead. Strewn around the clearing was a hodgepodge of dilapidated, burned out remains of tanks and armored vehicles bearing the scars of repeated bombings, strafings, and attacks by the forces from Hurlburt Field and adjoining Eglin Air Force Base. Dilapidated and burned, yet, in the dark they appeared menacingly real. For tonight's mission they represented the hostile forces arranged against our "customer" on the ground.

With the Pave Low beginning its evasive maneuvers, the pilots tersely informed the gunners, "Two minutes to target," and "Our customers are on the left, hostiles on the right," or "Your target is a column of tanks at our two o'clock position."

Immediately, the gunners responded over the intercom, "Right gun going hot," and "Tail gun going hot," indicating the tail gunner was arming his .50 caliber machine gun as both were awaiting visual acquisition of the targets.

Over the din of the jet engines powering the six huge rotor blades and the rush of the exhaust gusting through the open windows, the helicopter reverberated with the buzz-saw sound of the minigun quickly joined by the distinctive low-pitched pop-pop-pop of the .50 caliber machine gun. The deadly stream of tracers from the minigun looked as if a ribbon of fire were snaking its way to the target. At a rate of 4000 rounds per minute the interspersed tracer rounds appeared to be an uninterrupted stream of destruction.

As the right gun pressed his attack, the cacophony increased as the tail gunner, firing the .50 caliber machine gun, "walked" his rounds into the targets. The tracers slashed off into the darkness. While the helicopter jinked and banked, the gunners' aims remained steady as their rounds at first struck high or low then edged directly onto the targets. Since they had no optically enhanced gun sights or fancy heads-up-display (HUD) systems, their skill and accuracy under constantly changing circumstances was even more impressive.

As the Pave Low swept past the column of vehicles, streams of tracers converged on the rusted tank hulls. Some tracer rounds crazily ricocheted into the air as they impacted the armored vehicles. Others bounced and skipped along the ground.

In a matter of seconds we were out of range. Looking aft, past the lowered rear ramp, the scene was repeating itself as our wingman made his firing pass and joined the fray. Of course, the sound of its guns was drowned out by the ambient noise of our aircraft so that behind us appeared a slow-motion mime of our attack. Only the silhouette of our wingman could be seen as its tracer rounds stabbed down into the night.

Attention quickly reverted to our aircraft as the pilots wheeled the Pave Low around in a tight turn. The horizon seemed to slant at a 45 degree angle as the pilots were suddenly in voice contact with our "customers" on the ground and were making a dash for the landing zone (LZ). The coordinates given by the squad leader on the ground were clear and concise, "You have hostiles at eleven o'clock." The pilots confirmed the location of the Rangers, and the huge helicopter settled down amidst a cloud of dust and debris as near the edge of the clearing as possible. Just beyond the tree line six ghostly figures suddenly appeared racing toward the Pave Low with their heads down and their weapons at ready. The main landing gear had just touched down when the Rangers sprinted aboard. With the tail gunner confirming the last of the "customers" aboard, the Pave Low surged off into the night. Weighed down with rucksacks and weapons, the Rangers huddled on their knees as their squad leader shouted and gestured further instructions.

We flew evasive maneuvers for what seemed like an hour but in reality was only 10 to 15 minutes. We once again hovered over a new LZ, dropped off our "customers;" and as they disappeared into the darkened woods, we lifted off for other repeated attacks aimed at the vehicles below.

The training missions I accompanied were admittedly less hazardous than real world scenarios because no one was shooting back. One gunner flatly stated, "Our training is so realistic the only difference in combat is the adrenaline and fear you feel in the midst of hostile fire."

The AIR COMMANDOS book is an attempt to highlight the men and women of AFSOC and their unique capabilities. AFSOC is the vital link that allows special operations forces to infiltrate far behind enemy lines. Their systems and aircraft, including MC-130 Combat Talon, HC-130 Combat Shadow, EC-130E Commando Solo, MH-53J Pave Low, MH-60G Pave Hawk, and the AC-130 Spectre gunship are some of the most uniquely specialized aircraft in the world. No matter how impressive or sophisticated the aircraft or systems may be, AIR COMMANDOS is a people story. The highly motivated and superbly trained individuals of AFSOC add a new dimension to the word, teamwork. Each individual depends on the others for survival. Flight crews bet their lives on the fact that maintenance technicians have dutifully and conscientiously readied the aircraft for flight. Pilots depend on gunners and flight engineers as their extra sets of eyes as well as defenders of the aircraft. Navigators and Flight Control Officers rely on the sensor operators to distinguish between friendly and hostile forces who, in a fire fight, are only separated by a few dozen yards. The special tactics Combat Control Teams (CCTs) and Pararescuemen (PJs) owe their survival to the courage and tenacity of the gunship and helicopter crews. Other special operations forces depend heavily on the CCTs and PJs for expert guidance to and from the target and for trauma care when the shooting starts.

My experiences working with the Air Force Special Operations Command cannot begin to compare to the exhaustive hours of training or the deadly realities of combat endured by the air commandos. The rigorous training exercises I have accompanied are indicative of those relentlessly pursued around the clock in all kinds of weather, in a variety of jungle, desert, and arctic conditions. The training is justifiably intense. It is a high-stress environment with no margin for error. Because of the realistic training, the AFSOC forces have performed flawlessly. They are very, very good at what they do! Their morale is understandably high.

Hopefully, in some small way, my photography will give the reader a glimpse of one of the finest, most proficient, self-reliant combat teams in today's military. This book is also a token of sincere thanks. Thanks, not just for being allowed to go along for the ride; but, more importantly, thanks for the countless acts of heroism, the often painful sacrifices, and the assurance that when duty calls – the Air Commandos will be there – any time, any place!

MC-130 COMBAT TALON

While the Spectre gunships and the armed helicopters of AFSOC capture many of the headlines, the Combat Talon is truly the behind the scenes workhorse of the special operations world. The problem in telling the Combat Talon story is that much of what they do is shrouded in secrecy and their exploits remain hidden in the "black world" of special ops.

What is known is that the Combat Talon is a highly modified version of the Lockheed C-130. Over the years the Talon's capabilities have evolved from lessons learned on numerous variants of C-130s in a wide range of hostile and clandestine environments. As a result, tactics and systems have been perfected and modernizations made to the Talon I and built in from the start with Talon II.

From 1964 through 1972 Project Thin Slice was initiated to support a classified Southeast Asia program called Heavy Chain. Initially two C-130s were modified for the program and their use pioneered many systems

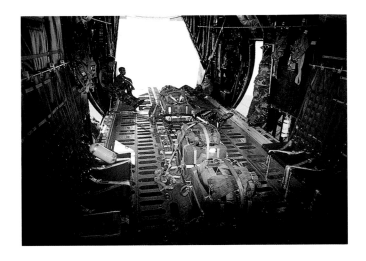

Facing Page:
MC-130H Combat Talon II of the 15th Special Operations Squadron, Hurlburt Field, Florida. Among the noticeable differences in appearance from the Combat Talon I, the bulbuous nose of the Talon II houses the AN/APQ-170 multi-mode radar.

Top:
Flightline maintenance crews take a quick break from the noonday sun while readying a Combat Talon for a night training mission. In the center of the cargo area are three bundles configured for the High Speed Low-Level Air Delivery System (HSLLADS). The Combat Talon can drop up to 2200 lbs in single or multi-bundle loads on each pass.

Bottom:
Flightline maintenance crews working on aircraft 1699 of the 15th Special Operations Squadron.

Facing Page:
Eventually, all Combat Talons will be painted in the all-gray low visibility scheme as sported by this MC-130E Talon I. However, the majority of the fleet remains in the green camouflage scheme.

Middle Photo, This Page:
An air-conditioning unit hooked up to an MC-130H Talon II keeps the avionics cool while operating on the ground.

that were later incorporated into the Combat Talon fleet; fuel tank baffling, High-Speed Low-Level Aerial Delivery System (HSLLADS), E-4 autopilot pitch channel monitor, Forward Looking Infrared system (FLIR), and electronic self-protection to improve survivability in the low to medium threat environment.

As the C-130E program was in full swing, several specialized "Skyhook" aircraft were produced. These aircraft differed from the standard C-130 in that they were equipped with the APQ-114 Terrain Following Radar, APS-54 Threat Warning System, and the Fulton Surface-to-Air Recovery System.

Also in the late 60s, training had begun for the initial "Stray Goose" crews to participate in Combat Spear missions based at Nha Trang Air Base, South Vietnam, by what was then the 15th Special Operations Squadron. It then became the 90th SOS until December 1972 when the unit became the 1st SOS based at Kadena AB, Japan. Much later, two crews from the 1st SOS participated in the Iranian Rescue Mission.

Combat Spear missions included combat personnel and supply drops as well as psyop materials drops throughout South Vietnam, Laos, Cambodia, and North Vietnam. During its time in Southeast Asia the unit lost two aircraft; one aircraft (64-547) crashed in Laos after a combat mission over North Vietnam, and the other aircraft (64-563) was destroyed in a mortar attack on Nha Trang AB in 1968.

This Page (top) and Pages 16 and 17:
MC-130E Combat Talon I of the 1st SOS on a low-level mission over the ocean. One aspect of the Talon's mission is to infiltrate special forces at night, over water, at extremely low altitudes using static-line air-drops of personnel and equipment including Zodiac inflatable boats.

Bottom:
MC-130E maintenance technician readying a 1st SOS aircraft for a training sortie. Note IRCM pod mounted on the underwing fuel tank.

During the late 60s, crews and modified C-130s also joined the 7th SOS in Germany where they conducted unconventional warfare duties in the USAFE area.

The 8th SOS, based at Hurlburt Field, FL was involved in the Son Tay Raid and the Iranian Rescue Mission. Currently the 8th SOS serves as the training squadron for the Talon I in addition to operational support of Air Force Special Operations Command around the world.

Since the late 60s and early 70s the MC-130E has evolved; modified with new mission capabilities, special ops equipment and electronics, enhancing its mission of penetrating hostile airspace at low altitudes at night or adverse weather in support of special operations forces.

The MC-130E Combat Talon I are flown by the 8th SOS at Hurlburt Field, FL and the 1st SOS based at Kadena AB, Japan.

With its integrated electronic countermeasures, highly accurate navigational system, FLIR, and terrain following/terrain avoidance radar the Talon crew is able to remain at a constant low altitude. Nine of the 14 Talon I aircraft still sport the Fulton Recovery System "whiskers" on the forward fuselage though the apparatus is used only in training. Though many have already been plumbed, eventually all MC-130E Talon I aircraft will be modified for helo-refueling where they can refuel helicopters

A Combat Talon I off the coast of Destin, Florida with Fort Walton Beach in the distant background.

With an MC-130H Combat Talon II on final approach in the background, an MC-130E Combat Talon I is readied for flight. Note the Fulton Recovery "whiskers" on the nose of the aircraft and the outboard underwing pods. The outboard underwing pods are for in-flight refueling of special operations helicopters – a mission shared with the HC-130P/N Combat Shadow (the MC-130Es are also plumbed as receivers for air-to-air refueling from KC-10 and KC-135 aircraft).

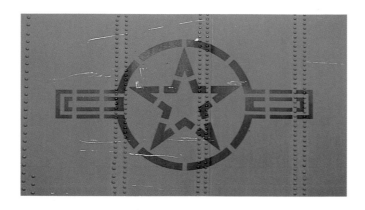

out of underwing refueling pods similar to the system used by Combat Shadow aircraft. With the Talon's proven low-level capabilities and upgraded electronics counter measures suite, it will be able to share in the refueling role currently performed by the HC-130N/P Combat Shadow. In addition to "passing gas" to special ops helicopters the Talon I can also be refueled by either KC-135 or KC-10, further extending its extremely long range capabilities.

By nature of the mission, special operations are designed to minimize the danger of enemy threats while maximizing natural advantages such as cover of darkness, surprise, and quickness. Or, as one pilot stated, "when going into bad guy country and they are waiting for you with a variety of weapons, particularly radar guided, there are two ways to go about it. First, you can enter overtly, while trying to suppress the threat with a variety of counter offensive weapons, such as the Wild Weasel, or

This Page (bottom):
For IR missile supression, the Talon carries a QRC-84-02A Infrared Countermeasure (IRCM) pod mounted on the underwing fuel tank on each side of the aircraft.

Facing Page:
Routine maintenance includes liquid oxygen (LOX) servicing (top left), checking engine intakes for foreign object damage (FOD) and inspecting landing gear area.

having an EF-111 along for company. The problem in this approach is that you are playing on their turf on their terms. The second approach is to sneak in and out, hopefully, without their ever knowing you were there. This approach presupposes that you have the ability to sneak. The best way to sneak is to take advantage of the factors not in their control, such as the terrain, and darkness." As a result, the Combat Talons are designed to come in fast and low at night to resupply and support ground forces by landing at austere locations or with precision high-speed drops – attracting as little attention as possible.

During DESERT STORM the MC-130E Combat Talon I carried out numerous psychological operations including the dispersement of leaflets as well as combat search and rescue missions. Out of the 27 combat sorties flown in DESERT STORM by the 8th SOS, five missions involved some of the more unusual bombing raids of the war. The Combat Talons were used to deliver the Air Force's largest conventional weapon; the 15,000 pound BLU-82. During the course of DESERT STORM, Combat Talons dropped a total of 11 BLU-82s which resulted in some of the most cataclysmic explosions of the war.

The concept of using the BLU-82 "Daisy Cutter" was first introduced by Lt. Colonel

The Fulton recovery system, though unorthodox, was designed as a safe method to rapidly recover personnel or equipment from either land or water. It involves the use of a large helium-filled balloon, a 450-foot nylon lift line and a protective suit and harness. The balloon, line, suit and harness are air-dropped and the person to be rescued puts on the suit, attaches one end of the nylon lift line to the harness and the other to the balloon. The balloon is then inflated and the lift line extended aloft. As the person waits for rescue, the aircraft flies over the rescue spot at 150 miles per hour, snags the lift line with scissor-like arms located on the aircraft's nose and reels in the human cargo through the lowered ramp in the back. Certainly a quick way to get out of tight spots in a hurry. On 24 August 1966, the first live surface-to-air recoveries of a one- and two-man pickups were accomplished. Although live pick-ups have not been done for years, 8th SOS crews still train for the mission.

Thomas Beres, 8th SOS Commander, around 20 January 1991. The Daisy Cutter is capable of destroying everything within a 300' radius and scatters shrapnel up to a mile; with a three foot nose fuse added, it explodes just high enough above the ground for the energy to be spread over the largest possible area. The standard procedure of dropping the bomb from 6,000 feet was deemed impractical due to the high threat intensity of AAA in the area. It was determined that the best and safest tactic would be to drop the bomb from 16,000 to 21,000 feet giving the aircrew better odds in evading the anticipated antiaircraft threats. It was further agreed to make multiple drops in order to increase the psychological impact on the enemy and to take advantage of the tactical surprise of the first bomb going off. In other words, as the enemy raised their heads to see what caused the first explosion – they would be exposed and caught unawares as the second one exploded. Each drop was given a force package comprised of EF-111, F-4G Wild Weasels, and EC-130 Compass Call which were employed to suppress and jam radar and communications.

Since General Schwarzkopf was interested in clearing mine fields situated opposite coalition ground forces, the first targets included mine fields and enemy troop concentrations. Though

the BLU-82 was used in Vietnam to create instant landing zones, no tests had ever been conducted regarding its effectiveness against mine fields.

On 3 February 1991, the first two of 18 BLU-82s arrived at King Fahd International Airport (KFIA) from Hill AFB, Utah. During the late night and early morning of 6/7 February 1991, an MC-130E Combat Talon I of the 8th SOS dropped the first BLU-82 on a mine field and blasted a safe passage through Iraqi defenses. The second bomb was dropped on an Iraqi battalion headquarters which resulted in the surrender of the commander, two intelligence officers, and a private. They reportedly cited the bombing as an influential factor in their surrender and promptly handed over detailed maps of adjacent mine fields.

The explosion of the Daisy Cutter in the southwest portion of Kuwait the night of 6/7 February created an enormous mushroom cloud. To many, it looked like "an atomic bomb detonating." The sound from the explosion carried for miles. A British SAS team, seeing the explosion from several miles away, reportedly radioed headquarters, "They've just nuked Kuwait."

The first BLU-82 drop appeared to be a success. Not only did the weapons reach their targets but all the aircrews returned safely. An unexpected bonus was realized when the Iraqis, interpreting the explosion as the beginning of the ground war, turned on their radars. An ill-advised move considering the number of HARM carrying coalition aircraft in the area!

On 14 February 1991 a double drop in the tri-border area resulted in massive enemy casualties.

The third BLU-82 mission occurred on 18 February when three MC-130E aircraft

Flightdeck crew of an MC-130E Combat Talon I of the 8th Special Operations Squadron. Right and left navigators (top left) at stations located on the right side of the aircraft, immediately behind the co-pilot (bottom). Note round gauges of Combat Talon I.

Opposite:
As pilots make final preparations to land at Hurlburt Field, the flight engineer (situated slightly behind the pilots) scans the airspace for traffic and is ready to assist the pilots in the event of an emergency.

approached Failaka Island from different directions and simultaneously dropped three Daisy Cutters. On the way to the target area all three aircraft encountered AAA fire. As the three bombs exploded (within five seconds of each other), all AAA fire ceased and within hours of detonation the island fell to coalition forces.

The fourth operation was targeted against two enemy division logistics points. On 20 February two Combat Talons delivered their bombs while navigating through violent thunderstorms, without radar, precisely on target from 21,000 feet. One of the bombs was dropped in a mine-strewn wadi deep inside Kuwait suspected of being the first line of defense for the Iraqi army. Immediate bomb damage assessment was unavailable due to the weather. Later, however, as U.S. soldiers arrived on the scene they encountered no enemy soldiers. Further along the second line of defense "there were lots of Iraqis – dead in their foxholes."

The fifth and final drop occurred on 22 February, one day before G-Day, and was another double drop – this time in support of U.S. Marine

(DOD photo)

Above:
The BLU-82, 15,000 lb. general purpose bomb. Eleven BLU-82s were dropped by Combat Talons on Iraqi positions during Operation DESERT STORM with devastating results.

Below:
Many of the analog controls and dials on other C-130s are incorporated into the MC-130H Combat Talon II's visual display terminals (VDTs). Two VDTs are in front of each flight deck crewmember (less the flight engineer) and display all flight director, navigation, radio control, flight plan, fuel/power management, and equipment status information. The displays also allow radar and infrared video to be overlaid onto various digital display formats. All controls and displays on the flight deck are completely night vision goggle (NVG) compatible. This integration allows each crewmember direct access to all mission essential controls in two easy to reach VDTs.

The round gauges in the center of the console are engine related instruments. The throttle controls and condition levers for the props are shown immediately below the engine gauges.

OUR NAME IS WRITTEN ALL OVER THEM

We're the leading edge in wings. And the last word in communications. We're the air you breath. And the muscle to stop the largest cargo plane. We're guidance and propulsion, avionics and hydraulics. Complete integrated systems and a whole lot more.

If it flies, it's a sure bet it's flying with us aboard. Fighter or bomber. Trainer or special mission. Even into outer space.

We're the business units of AlliedSignal Aerospace, the leading innovators in aerospace technology for over 60 years, who believe there's no substitute for experience. And no greater goal than 100% reliability and total customer satisfaction.

When you look to the future of aerospace, look around. There's a 99% probability we're already on board.

© 1993 AlliedSignal Inc.

nominated targets. At the end of hostilities the
seven remaining BLU-82s were destroyed at KFIA.

Putting bombs on target, by MC-130E
aircraft no less, was a tribute to efficiency,
coordination – and creativity of the crews and
the accuracy of their integrated on-board
mission systems.

The same high degree of accuracy in the
even more threatening environment a few
hundred feet off the ground is the norm while
resupplying special forces units. The high-speed,
low-level drop routine performed by the Combat
Talon crews accomplishes at least two tactical
objectives. Since the Talon does not "pop up" to
altitude to acquire and target the drop zone, it
does not compromise the location of the ground
forces. In the event enemy radar does track the
aircraft, they are not alerted to the whereabouts of
the drop zone as the Talon presents no anomalies
in the flight profile as it nears, flies over, and
egresses the area. By maintaining a fast, low-level
approach, Talon crews further minimize AAA
threats in the area. As one crew member has
said, "we're in and out of the drop zone so fast,
nobody knows we're there."

On the other hand, the Talon can fly at
such high altitudes as to be above most threats
and drop HAHO equipped jumpers several miles
from the drop zone, egressing the area long
before the parachute forces arrive at their

Previous Pages (28-29): An MC-130H Combat Talon II of the 15th Special Operations Squadron. The distinctive bulbous nose houses the AN/APQ-170 multi-mode radar. Immediately under the nose is the FLIR. The IRCM pod is mounted on an outboard pylon on each wing. The red boxes on the aft fuselage are chaff and flare dispensers.

This Page:
Practice makes perfect! Showing its low-level, high-speed airdrop capabilities in broad daylight, the Combat Talon's sophisticated mission system computer and navigation systems allow it to perform the same degree of accuracy at night or in poor weather.

Following Pages (32-33):
On an extremely low-level pass, an MC-130H of the 15th SOS releases three bundles precisely on target.

predetermined landing zones.

The MC-130H combat Talon II is an all new aircraft developed to augment the Talon I mission and is flown by the 15th SOS at Hurlburt Field, FL and the 7th SOS based at RAF Mildenhall, UK. Twenty-three Talon IIs have been delivered to the Air Force Special Operations Command and a 24th aircraft will be delivered by the end of 1994. With a crew of seven (two pilots, navigator, electronic warfare officer, flight engineer, and two loadmasters) the Talon II performs day or night, adverse weather, low-level operations to deliver troops and supplies to enemy denied areas.

The Combat Talon II has an upgraded, user friendly flight deck featuring an integrated avionics mission system which combines basic aircraft flight data, tactical data and mission sensor data into a comprehensive array of display formats. All these upgrades greatly improve situational awareness and crew coordination since most missions take place in the high-stress environment of low-level nighttime/adverse weather flying. The flight deck and cargo area are night vision goggle compatible giving the crew the flexibility of monitoring the flight controls and keeping an eye outside the cockpit simultaneously.

The bulbous nose of the MC-130H houses the AN/APQ-170 multi-mode radar which provides redundant terrain-following/terrain avoidance, weather detection and ground mapping capabilities and has a "look into turn"

Previous Pages (34-35):
As the Combat Talon approaches the drop zone, the loadmasters make last minute inspections to ensure that the bundles to be dropped are configured and loaded properly. With pre-programmed coordinates from the mission system computer, the High Speed Low Level Air Delivery System (HSLLADS) automatically catapults the load off the ramp and out of the aircraft. Lower photo page 35 features a heavy equipment load.

This Page:
Due to the extremely low altitude and high speed of the airdrop, the parachutes deploy immediately. The accuracy of the HSLLADS system is clearly demonstrated in the lower photograph.

With their MC-130E Combat Talon I in the background, an 8th Special Operations Squadron aircrew compare notes and begin unloading personal gear after a 4.5 hour training mission. Though the normal crew consists of two pilots, two navigators, electronic warfare officer, flight engineer, communications specialist, and two loadmasters, training flights are often crowded with alternate crewmembers and instructors.

The above photograph clearly shows the MC-130H Combat Talon II's distinctive radome, the white in-flight refueling markings on top of the fuselage, and the IDS turret located directly under the nose.

Combat Talon crews are able to "see" obstacles or barriers at night with the aid of the IDS, and Night Vision Goggles (NVG) and land safely at blacked out or austere runways. Because of the elongated nose configuration, the Talon II IDS turret remains operable during landing while the Talon I must retract its FLIR turret to deconflict with the landing gear door.

capability allowing the aircraft to follow terrain contours even during a turn. The infrared detection set (IDS) can be slewed to flight path vectors and helps the pilots visually clear terrain and avoid threat areas. The Texas Instruments-developed FLIR system provides an extremely high quality image of terrain features and, combined with the radar map and other systems, gives the crew an accurate picture of the flight path.

The mission computer, which helps the aircraft stay low and fast at night also helps the crew accurately drop supplies to special operations forces with reliable precision. The load and ballistics parameters are factored into the mission computer prior to take off and updated by the navigation systems once in the air. The pilots use the radar and FLIR to designate the drop zone and, once coordinates in the computer line up, the load is automatically catapulted out of the aircraft settling precisely on target.

With the ability to resupply forces on the ground, or to actually infiltrate special forces teams from either extremely low or high altitudes, the Combat Talons and their crews continue to be a vital link in AFSOCs far reaching unconventional warfare missions.

Having just released its load of supplies for the special operations forces on the ground, an 8th SOS MC-130E Combat Talon I streaks for home. This particular aircraft sports the Fulton Recovery System "whiskers" mounted on the nose and features two outboard underwing refueling pods for air-to-air refueling of special operations helicopters.

MC-130

AC-130

HC-130

Lockheed
Aircraft Service Company

For more than 30 years we have met the test to provide timely mission – capable systems, modifications and installations for Air Commando operators. We help make the concept "Any time, any place" a reality.

EC-130

EC-130E COMMANDO SOLO

Several C-130E aircraft have been modified and designated EC-130E (Rivet Rider modification) to support psychological operations. The Commando Solo aircraft are flown by the 193rd Special Operations Group (Pennsylvania Air National Guard) based at Harrisburg International Airport, PA., and operate

193rd has participated in practically every combat action including Vietnam, Grenada, Panama and Southwest Asia.

The primary mission of the 193rd SOG and its EC-130E aircraft is to transmit radio and television broadcasts to the enemy's military and civilian population. During Operation JUST CAUSE EC-130Es transmitted messages not only interrupting General Noriega's televised broadcasts, but also encouraged civilians to stay

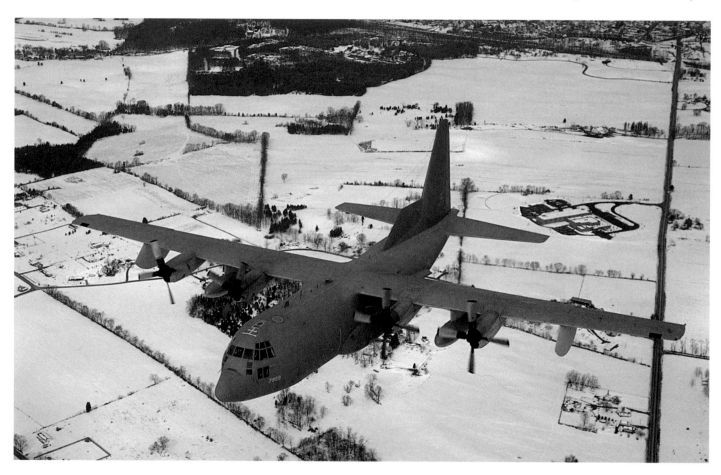

under the command of AFSOC at Hurlburt Field. The 193rd is the only Air National Guard unit with a special operations mission.

The 193rd has a rich heritage dating back to 1947. In the late 1960s the unit converted to the EC-121 "Super Constellation" and created what has become one of the most distinguished flying units in the Air Force. In 1977, the 30th anniversary of the unit, eight C-130E aircraft were received. In March, 1979, the unit received the first of four EC-130Es and in May retired the last operational EC-121. Since the early 1970s the

at home and away from the conflict. One mission, which included air refueling, lasted 21 hours.

During Operation DESERT STORM, working with U.S. Army psychological operations units, appeals were broadcast encouraging Iraqi tank crews to surrender and abandon their vehicles. Other psyop missions supported leaflet drops and included broadcasts of prayers from the Koran and messages from well-treated prisoners extolling the availability of food and medical supplies. Likewise, messages were broadcast describing the dire consequences to

*Aircraft #7869 then and now. Converted EC-130s arrived at the 193rd
Special Operations Group in March, 1979 in the Southeast Asia
camouflage paint scheme. The low visibility gray scheme will
eventually be standard on all the unit's aircraft.*

befall any who refused to surrender.

The 193rd SOG initially deployed two EC-130Es to the Southwestern Asia theater at the outset of Operation DESERT SHIELD. These two aircraft accumulated over 500 flying hours in a matter of weeks and accomplished 99 percent of their tasked missions. In January, 1991, a third EC-130E deployed to a second location in the region as the 193rd partially mobilized (having previously met mission tasking with volunteers on 30-45 day rotations) and maintained a 100 percent availability rate throughout its deployment. During DESERT STORM the unit's aircrews averaged more than 14 flying hours per day for 60 consecutive days and far exceeded its wartime tasking. Maintenance crews generated aircraft at an unprecedented rate of 289 percent above their normal level. During their time in the Saudi desert the 193rd also achieved another milestone – 130,000 hours of accident-free flying.

In January, 1992 the 193rd deployed to Wake Island to work with USAF officials, Lockheed Aircraft Services (Ontario) and Rockwell-Collins to test the world-wide color television capabilities of the EC-130E. Upon the successful completion of the deployment, aircraft 9817 (unofficially christened "Starship 9817" because of its modified appearance) returned home after an absence of almost three years of modification and testing.

In its peacetime role the Commando Solo provides emergency radio and television broadcast capabilities for civilian areas ravaged by natural disasters, such as hurricanes or earthquakes, where local transmitters are damaged or destroyed.

The Commando Solo normally carries a crew of 11 (two pilots, navigator, electronic warfare officer, flight engineer, loadmaster, and five electronic equipment operators). While airborne, the psyop mission is coordinated by the mission control chief working with the operators involved with both search and transmission duties. Mission transmitters include medium-frequency (MF), high-frequency (HF), very high-frequence (VHF) and ultra high-frequency (UHF). Output power is from 10 watts to 10 kilowatts. Modes of operation include AM/FM radio, black and white and color television, shortwave and other communications bands. The Commando Solo also has the capability to disrupt standard broadcasts. Signals can be broadcast from either side of the aircraft depending on the location of the target audience.

The EC-130E(R) is clearly discernable in appearance from other variants of the C-130. Two versions of the EC-130E are flown by the 193rd. The older version is recognizable by the large blade antenna on the upper fuselage adjoining the tail fin and scimitar-shaped blade antennas outboard under each wing. Two air

(DOD photo)

52

The 193rd Special Operations Group was the first Air National Guard flying squadron formed in Pennsylvania after World War II. The unit has flown the P-47, P-51, C-46, C-119 and the "Super Constellation" C/EC-121 prior to taking delivery of the EC-130E. The last C-121 was retired to Davis-Monthan AFB, AZ in March, 1979.

The lower photograph was taken during the 30th Anniversary year of the 193rd SOG, 1977, as the EC-121 was leaving and the new EC-130s were arriving. Note that the EC-130E parked in the background is none other than "Starship 9817" pictured above — newly modified and the most advanced EC-130E Commando Solo in the Air Force.

Above:
A low level pass over the Susquehanna River and Harrisburg, Pennsylvania.

Right:
The latest version of the EC-130E Commando Solo is easily recognized by the four bullet-shaped VHF antenna on the tail fin and the two underwing pods (each 6 ft. in diameter and 23 ft. long) housing rotatable high-frequency antennas. The pod directly below the tail fin houses a retractable trailing-wire antenna which can be extended in flight several hundred feet behind the aircraft.

conditioning condenser pods, located on each side of the fuselage, dissipate heat generated by the electronic equipment. The latest model of the EC-130E(R), with its worldwide color television broadcast capabilities, is easily recognized by the four missile-shaped VHF antenna located on the tail fin and the two large, 23-ft. long, 6-ft. diameter pods suspended under each outboard

Much of what the Commando Solo does is classified. Its missions are largely concealed in secrecy. What is known, however, is that the aircraft has performed beyond expectations and has reliably accomplished its mission taskings. The success of any aircraft, however, is largely dependent on the quality work of the people who fly, maintain and support it. The citizen warriors

wing section. The tail mounted VHF antennas are for lower-frequency television channels while the rotatable antennas in the wing pods are dedicated to higher-frequency television channels. There are two retractable trailing-wire antennas; a high-frequency (HF) antenna that is trailed out horizontally several hundred feet behind the aircraft and a 1,000-ft. AM-band omnidirectional antenna extended from the belly of the aircraft, held in a near-vertical position by a 500-lb. weight.

of the 193rd have consistently displayed an integrity of spirit and a keen understanding of their duty as evidenced in the number of Safety, Operational Readiness, and Air Force Outstanding Unit awards accumulated over the years. Their willingness to respond and readiness to perform is a tribute to the professionalism of everyone involved with Air Force Special Operations Command. The 193rd Special Operations Group is truly the "Voice of the Quiet Professionals" of AFSOC.

Across the Spectrum, Around the Globe –

Information – how and when you want it ...

HC-130 COMBAT SHADOW

One of the primary reasons Pave Low and Pave Hawk helicopters have performed "as advertised" in recent conflicts, travelling long distances at night to arrive at specific destinations with precision, is their ability to refuel enroute in the air. Take away the in-flight refueling capabilities and the MH-53, MH-60, MH-47 and

The Combat Shadow is a highly modified version of the C-130 missionized for special operations. The self contained navigation systems include an inertial system (INS) and a global positioning systems (GPS). With its infrared detection set (IDS) and night vision goggle (NVG) heads up display the crew can "see" and fly in the dark. In fact, all interior and exterior lighting is NVG compatible. The upgraded communications include a data burst device and satellite

MH-60K, the helicopters are severly limited in range and restricted considerably in what they can accomplish. The Pave Low, even with auxiliary tanks, has an operational range of about 700 miles. The AFSOC asset that supports the helicopters and gives them such "long legs" is the HC-130P/N Combat Shadow.

Combat Shadow aircraft are flown by crews of the 9th SOS at Hurlburt Field, FL., the 67th SOS at RAF Mildenhall, U.K., the 17th SOS at Kadena AB, Japan, and the 542nd CTW at Kirtland AFB, NM.

communications capabilities. Threat detection and countermeasures include radar and missile warning systems and chaff and flare dispensers.

Most HC-130P/N are also Universal Aerial Refueling Receptacle Slipway Installation (UARRSI) modified so that they can be refueled in flight by KC-135 and KC-10 aircraft. With their extended loiter capabilities they are truly force multipliers as fewer HC-130P/Ns are required to support large helo deployments, employments, and redeployments.

Since its first flights in 1964, the Combat Shadow has served during several conflicts in a variety of roles; search and rescue, command and control, and its current role as an airborne refueler for special forces helicopters.

The entire fleet of HC-130P/N aircraft is in the process of being modified with Global Positioning System (GPS), FLIR, radar warning recievers, NVG compatible heads-up display and in-flight refueling capabilities as a receiver.

The crew is able to update their position using IDS, radar, and GPS. With the improved navigation, communications, threat detection, and countermeasures systems they are able to provide refueling support and airdrop or airland special forces teams and their equipment for both ground and water operations in the low to medium threat environment.

The crew consists of a pilot and copilot, two navigators, flight engineer, communications systems operator, and two loadmasters.

The Combat Shadow carries enough supplemental fuel to arrive at and return from the target area and loiter overhead if required with enough on-board fuel to "drag" the receivers to their appointed destinations and back. The Combat Shadow can refuel two helicopters simultaneously; one on each side from the drogue-and-probe baskets extended from the air refueling pods mounted under each wing outboard of engines #1 and #4.

Air to air refueling is an exact business regardless of the aircraft involved (whether it's KC-135 or KC-10 refueling fighters at 20,000 feet or Combat Shadows refueling helicopters at 500 feet). The fact that two or more aircraft are flying several hundred miles an hour only a few yards apart requires great skill, patience and nerves of steel. Since the 1950s the Air Force has pioneered and mastered in-flight refueling and has truly multiplied the impact of its forces through the proficiency of their air refueling crews and receivers. That is certainly the case

Following Page:
As an HC-130P/N Combat Shadow holds a straight and level course, an MH-53J Pave Low nears the basket for refueling.

with the contributions made by the Combat Shadow crews.

The conditions under which they refuel are extremely demanding and require considerable concentration and effort. Normally both the Combat Shadow and the receiving helicopters fly "blacked out" – with no formation lights or radio communication. Without night vision goggles the entire scenario would be virtually impossible. Precision flying and accurate navigation are essential for the Combat Shadow to rendezvous with the helicopters. As the Combat Shadow crew visually acquires its receivers, the pilots gain altitude in order to overfly the helicopter and maintain a level course at a constant speed of around 110 knots – the absolute minimum for the fuel laden aircraft. The helicopter crew, through the use of their NVGs, acquire visual contact on the tanker and increase their speed and altitude, catching up with the tanker, flying very tight formation. As the helicopter tucks into position, its main rotor is only a few feet away from the trailing edge of the tanker's horizontal stabilizer. The refueling basket, trailed from a hose attached to the outboard refueling pod, is eventually "plugged" by the extended refueling probe of the helicopter. Frequently two helicopters are refueled at the same time and, more often than not, the scene is repeated several times as the tight formation ingresses and egresses the target area.

The sorties flown by the HC-130P/N are single or multi-ship, low-level, nighttime missions every bit as gruelling and dangerous as the helicopter mission. Their defense against enemy threats is much the same as the helicopters; be unpredictable, fly low, and fly at night.

This Page:
HC-130P/N Combat Shadows during Operation DESERT STORM.

Opposite Page:
With rotor blades only a few feet away from the tail surfaces of the Combat Shadow, the refueling process requires concentration and superb airmanship.

(DOD photo)

In practically every instance where special operations forces have been called upon, Combat Shadows have supported the effort. In August 1989 HC-130N crews from the 9th SOS at Hurlburt augmented HC-130s of the 67th SOS in support of four MH-60G Pave Hawk helicopters of the 20th SOS in the humanitarian effort to locate Congressman Mickey Leland's aircraft missing in Ethiopia. The Combat Shadows and Pave Hawks flew over 460 hours in support of the search mission.

In Operation JUST CAUSE six HC-130s participated (three from the 9th SOS and three from the 542nd Combat Crew Training Wing at Kirtland AFB, NM). Prior to H-Hour Combat Shadow crews were part of a 12-hour mission

(DOD photo)

refueling Pave Lows flying non-stop from Hurlburt to Panama. As Operation DESERT STORM began, the 9th SOS was already airborne providing tanker support for the Pave Lows guiding the Army AH-64 Apaches as part of Task Force Normandy. The 67th SOS, operating out of Incirlik Air Base, Turkey was already in place providing support from the north. HC-130 Combat Shadows also supported MH-60G Pave Low operations in Saudi Arabia's eastern province. Throughout DESERT STORM the 9th SOS and 67th SOS Combat Shadow crews joined up with the helicopters often from 25 to 75 miles into Iraq to pass enough gas for their safe return to base.

The nighttime operations over the desert were particularly hazardous as on some missions it was so dark that helicopter pilots had difficulty seeing the refueling baskets. An in-the-field "fix" included infrared "peanut" lights affixed to the basket and the hose so that from the air the helicopter crews could acquire visual contact with the basket and plug in to refuel.

In addition to refueling duties, the Combat Shadow crews performed CSAR and special operations airlift and eventually logged over 300 flying hours in 103 DESERT STORM sorties.

Much of the success of today's special operations is a result of the cohesive, self-reliant nature of their mission, assets and people. Unlike in ages past, when one service had to beg, borrow and steal people and aircraft, AFSOC is a well trained, highly organized, and proficient strike

force able to respond anywhere in the world on short notice in support of special forces teams. A vital element of that quick response capability is the contribution made by the Combat Shadow crews. Their airborne support and refueling efforts give AFSOC the unrestricted flexibility to act quickly and safely return home with the mission accomplished.

To you, it looks like a rainy
night with no visibility.
To a Special Operations
Commando,
it looks like an anti-aircraft
missile site 12 miles ahead
and a mountain range
off to the left.

Moonless nights and bad weather are normal flying conditions when you're a member of the U.S. Special Operations Command. It takes nerves of steel and tremendous skill to fly in conditions like these.

It also takes extraordinarily sophisticated avionics systems.

For more than two decades, Loral Federal Systems has taken pride in helping these dedicated warriors complete hundreds of successful covert missions. By creatively integrating a wide range of sensor, communication, navigation, and display technologies into unusually powerful, workload-reducing avionic systems, we've given the Special Operations crews the threat avoidance and mission management capabilities they need to fulfill their missions without being detected.

These Commandos risk their lives to protect the interests of our country. They deserve the best support they can get.

LORAL
Federal Systems

MH-53J PAVE LOW III

The Sikorsky MH-53J Pave Low III helicopter is big by any standards; 92 feet long, 23 feet wide and 17 feet high, topped by six titanium rotor blades, casting a 72 ft. shadow. Powered by two General Electric T64-GE-100 engines, its maximum gross weight is 50,000 lbs. for combat operations.

The six man crew consists of two pilots, two flight engineers and two gunners. One engineer occupies a jump seat mounted between the pilot and copilot and assists the pilots, operating the navigational systems, while the other operates the right side machine gun (and rescue hoist) mounted in the window just aft of the forward bulkhead. One of the gunners operates the machine gun mounted in the left window and the other gunner is stationed on the ramp at the rear of the aircraft.

The MH-53J is equipped with armor plating and three machine guns. Depending on the type of mission flown, the armament can be either 7.62mm miniguns or .50 caliber machine guns – or a combination of both.

The Pave Low is arguably the most sophisticated helicopter in the world. It is ideally suited for the rugged tasks of nighttime special operations and provides AFSOC with an adverse all-weather, heavy lift capability currently unmatched by any other rotary wing platform in the U.S. inventory.

(DOD photo)

Though the Pave Low is noted for toughness and durability, its highly sophisticated navigation and night flying avionics put it in a class by itself. The forward looking infrared systems (FLIR) and the terrain-following/terrain-avoidance (TF/TA) radar are fully integrated with the on-board mission computer. Combined with the ring laser gyro (RLG), inertial navigation system (INS), global positioning system (GPS), and doppler navigation system, the Pave Low is capable of flying very low mission profiles at night in adverse weather to arrive at a precise location at a specific time.

The Pave Low airframe is not new. It is a highly modified version of the HH-53 Super Jolly Green Giant helicopter used extensively in Southeast Asia for special operations and rescue of combat personnel. Under the Air Force's Pave Low IIIE program, 41 MH-53Hs and CH-53s were modified for night and adverse weather operations and subsequently designated MH-53Js. Many of the systems on the Pave Low incorporate off-the-shelf technology. The projected map display and radar, for example, are from the A-7 while the ring laser gyro INS was originally developed for use with the space shuttle program.

Up close the MH-53J is huge and its brute strength readily apparent. The aft portion of the Pave Low resembles a medium size cargo aircraft rather than a helicopter. It can transport 36 fully equipped troops while the external cargo hook has a 20,000 pound capacity. The large ramp at the rear of the aircraft remains in the level position throughout flight to provide easy on-off access and acts as a permanent platform for the pedestal mounted machine gun. From his perch on the ramp the tail gunner has almost a 180 degree field of fire.

Up front, on the flightdeck, the cockpit is a

Top:
Key members of the Pave Low team are the avionics technicians maintaining the APQ-158 TF/TA radar.

Left:
A 20th Special Operations Squadron "Green Hornet" prepares to taxi at Hurlburt Field, Florida.

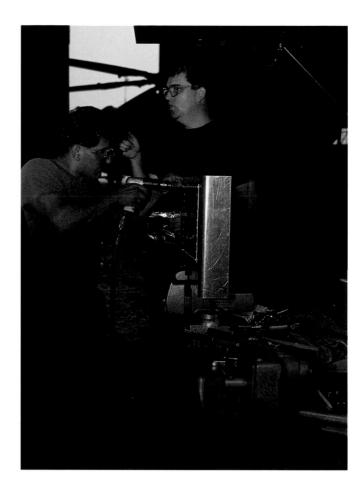

While routine maintenance takes place out on the flightline, each aircraft is scheduled for major repairs and overhauling based on hours flown.

Top Left:
After the helicopter has been painted in the low-visibility gray, all the stencils and warning signs have to be reapplied.

Top Right:
In-house metal fabrication allows the Air Force to build and repair special modifications for new equipment.

Bottom:
Paint booth where engine nacelles are being masked and spray painted.

Facing Page:
Isochronal inspections are performed periodically for preventative maintenance.

myriad of avionics and navigation displays which include the terrain-following/terrain-avoidance radar, FLIR and moving map displays. In flight, the radar paints a high resolution picture, clearly showing any obstacles in the flight path. The FLIR shows a video-like image of the landscape in the helicopter's path, only instead of light it "sees" heat. On the FLIR display, critical flight data is superimposed including horizon, altitude, groundspeed, and flight direction. The moving

Top:
A maintenance technician has the nose compartment door open and has access to the ALQ-162 jammer, C-12 compass gyro, hover coupler amplifier, Automatic Flight Control System (AFCS), and the turn rate gyro.

Middle and Facing Pages:
Because the Pave Low works in a dirty, dusty environment performing its mission, the combination of dust, grime from jet engine exhaust, sand and any number of other corrosives must be removed. The wash rack is not a glamorous job – but a necessary one.

map display is a great tool for situational awareness providing an accurate representation of the aircraft's location. The cockpit lighting is specially modified to allow the pilots to fly at night using night vision goggles (NVGs) and not be blinded by the lights of the instruments. The TF/TA radar, FLIR and NVGs allow the pilots to fly the Pave Low at ground hugging altitudes in total darkness.

In addition to the sophisticated terrain avoidance avionics, the Pave Low incorporates a hover coupler system which helps stabilize the helicopter during hovering – not an easy task anytime – but especially difficult at night over water, in poor visibility or in the middle of a fire fight. The Pave Lows' hover coupler system is engaged a few miles prior to the landing zone and the system processes signals from gyroscopes, a radar altimeter and the helicopter's inertial guidance system to maintain a steady hover. Almost like an automatic pilot system,the hover coupler system guides the aircraft to the landing zone and allows the pilot to hold a preselected altitude, above a preprogrammed point on the ground.

The Air Force Special Operations Command has four squadrons equipped with the MH-53J III Pave Low; the 20th Special Operations Squadron (SOS) based at Hurlburt Field, Florida, the 21st SOS based at RAF Mildenhall, U.K., the 31st SOS based at Osan Air Base, Korea and the 551st SOS based at Kirtland AFB, New Mexico where Pave Low crews receive initial qualification training.

The primary mission of the MH-53J is to provide long-range insertion, resupply and exfiltration of special forces teams well behind enemy lines and to perform combat personnel recovery operations for SOF assets. The Pave Low is well suited to these missions and they are practiced relentlessly at Hurlburt, Mildenhall, and Osan and routinely employed throughout the world by all Pave Low squadrons. Since the Pave Low is in-flight refuelable and has an enormous payload, it gives the special forces community increased options for taking the war to the enemy far behind the front lines.

Most of the training for the Pave Low crews takes place at night, nearly always in joint exercises with other special forces troops, and in as realistic environments as possible.

The U.S. Air Force is firmly committed to the philosophy of "fighting the way we train", so AFSOCs training duplicates as near as possible the ways they intend to fight. The investment in such realistic training paid huge dividends in both Operation JUST CAUSE and DESERT STORM.

From 17 December 1989 to 3 January 1990, approximately 500 personnel from the 23rd Air Force (now known as Air Force Special Operations Command) participated in Operation JUST CAUSE, the action against the Panamanian forces of General Manuel Noriega. The plan in Panama called for 27 separate and simultaneous raids, airdrops or attacks against eleven different locations. H-Hour was at 0045 Panama time on 20 December 1989. In addition to five MH-53Js from the 20th SOS, three MC-130E (8th SOS); two AC-130A (711th SOS); seven AC-130H (16th SOS); four MH-60G (55th SOS); three HC-130P/N (9th SOS); three HC-130P/N (1550th CCTW); and two HC-130E (193rd SOG) participated in the action. The five Pave Lows were flown from Hurlburt Field to Panama for the operation. The

Opposite, Top:
The sheer size of the Pave Low, with its 72 ft. diameter rotor, makes inspection a challenge. The flight engineer inspects the elastomeric main rotor head (ERH). The ERH can be folded for full shipboard compatibility.

Opposite, Middle:
An ALQ-157 IR jammer is carried on each side of the helicopter mounted on the sponson just above the drop tank.

Opposite, Bottom:
The SX-5E Controllable Infrared (IR) Light is a 500 watt zenon lamp that provides a high intensity source of light. These were used extensively in DESERT SHIELD/DESERT STORM because it was so dark in the desert – especially when there was a lot of dust in the air. The dust seemed to soak up any illumination and, as one pilot not so jokingly stated ". . . it made brave, macho men not so brave and macho." A sentiment not hard to imagine when flying so close to the featureless desert at night.

deployed flight took over twelve hours and required three inflight refuelings from HC-130 Combat Shadow aircraft. Pave Low crews performed distinguished duty in numerous hostile engagements including the resupply, reinforcement and evacuation of Navy SEALS at Paitilla Airport.

The value of intense, realistic training again paid off during DESERT STORM when Pave Low crews were able to make immediate contributions to the success of the air campaign.

During DESERT SHIELD a plan was drawn

special forces ground personnel in the event of casualities or if their exfiltration helicopters were shot down.

Due to the complexity of putting special forces teams on the ground, behind enemy lines, several days in advance of the strike and the lack of GPS (global positioning system) man packs in the theater, INSTANT THUNDER was cancelled pending a more reliable plan.

In the interim, the Iraqis moved the radar sites back from three or four miles from the border to between 20 and 40 miles.

up, code name INSTANT THUNDER, where members of the 5th Special Forces Group (SFG) would attack three radar sites located on the northwest border of Saudi Arabia with Iraq in order to open a hole in the radar coverage which would allow coalition aircraft to pour through undetected. The 3rd Battalion of the 160th SOAR was tasked with getting the special forces teams out once they destroyed the radar sites. The 20th SOS, with their Pave Lows,were assigned the task of CSAR (Combat Search And Rescue) for any strike aircraft going down in Iraq and for any

Since the task of knocking out the radar sites was essential to the success of the air campaign, General Schwarzkopf asked his staff who was available for the job and who had GPS to do the mission "right away?" Colonel Johnson at SOCCENT responded that the only aircraft with GPS "are the Pave Lows of the 20th SOS". While the 20th SOS could certainly reach the targets at a precise time in the no-moon blackness, the lack of heavy fire power (being armed with only their side firing and ramp .50 caliber machine guns) left some question as to whether they could totally

A 20th SOS helicopter painted in desert camouflage about to be "air mailed" to one of the world's hot spots. Two MH-53Js can be loaded into the C-5.

Ultimately, it's a people business. The most sophisticated equipment in the world is only as good as the pilots, gunners and maintainers.

Top Left:
A Pave Low pilot steps to his aircraft.

Top Right:
An MH-53J gunner carrying the thick fast-rope used by special operations forces to quickly repel from the helicopter. Note also the flight helmet and carrying case containing the night vision goggles.

Bottom:
A gunner/flight engineer listens and intently looks for any malfunctions just prior to take-off.

Opposite:
The team work exhibited by Pave Low crews adds new meaning to the term "crew coordination". Here a crew reviews their objectives during a mission briefing.

knock out the Iraqi communications so that even a phone call would not get out.

The suggestion was made to include Army AH-64 Apaches to bring to bear enough fire power to ensure immediate and total success. Training for the mission, code named TASK FORCE NORMANDY, was initiated during the second week of October 1990 with Pave Lows and Apaches working as a combined strike package. They worked together once a week for four weeks. During that time they coordinated their tactics for formation and communications procedures and became accustomed to working closely together. The Pave Low and Apache crews quickly became proficient in complimenting each other's strengths. The plan to take out the radar sites was rehearsed repeatedly, including live fire exercises with the Hellfire missiles on the Saudi King Fahd range.

By mid October, intelligence sources confirmed that the radar sites had been moved 23 miles inside Iraq and had been consolidated from three sites into two.

The original plan for hitting the three radar sites called for three formations each with three Apaches and one Pave Low. Once the radar sites were consolidated, the plan was altered to include two formations each of four Apaches and two Pave Lows. The ninth Apache flew as an alternate in the event one of the other eight malfunctioned en route to the targets. In each formation one Pave Low served as lead and the other flew alternate lead with back up navigation and CSAR duties.

The mission with the eight Apaches and four Pave Lows was to blast several Soviet designed radar units including the "Spoon Rest" mobile early warning radar, the "Flat Face" early warning and target acquisition radar, and the

"Squat Eye" search and target acquisition radar.

The mission required split second timing and instantaneous destruction of the two radar sites. The exchange between Colonel Gray, commander of the 1st Special Operations Wing and all Central Command Special Operations Air Forces and General Schwarzkopf has assumed almost legendary proportions. The general reportedly asked "are you going to guarantee me 100 percent success on this mission?" to which Colonel Gray responded "Yes, Sir". General Schwarzkopf's response ". . . then you get to start the war" must be one of the classic statements of modern warfare.

Confidence in success of the mission ran high. "This was the best joint helicopter flying operation I've ever seen," said Lt. Colonel Richard L. Comer, 20th SOS Commander, "the Apache was obviously made to shoot and destroy a target, and the Pave Low was made to take shooters to a target. Our job was to get the shooters to the target on time and the Apaches job was to kill the enemy."

The 20th SOS crews at Al Jouf received orders at about 1400 hours on 16 January 1991 to begin the air war. Time over target (TOT) was set for 22 minutes prior to H-hour. Briefing for

*Gunners and flight engineer load 7.62mm ammunition for the
two side firing mini-guns and, in this case ramp mounted
mini-gun as well. The standard load is 4,500 rounds per minigun
and 800 rounds per .50 caliber machine gun.*

the crews was set for 2200 hours with take off set for 0100 hours. Since the coalition fighters and bombers were scheduled to pour through the hole in radar coverage in northwestern Iraq by 0300 hours, there was no margin for error.

At 0212 hours the 13 aircraft of TASK FORCE NORMANDY crossed the border into Iraq. Captain Corby Martin's flight with Captain Ben Pulsifer's crew flying number two had the western most target while Captain Mike Kingsley with Major Bob Leonik piloting the helicopter on his wing had the eastern target. Lt. Colonel Comer flew with Major Leonik as copilot. The Army Battalion commander, Lt. Colonel Dick Cody, flew the trail Apache in the first formation led by Captain Kingsley. The night was pitch-black and the Pave Low crews relied totally on the computers and sensors in their cockpit flying no more than 50 feet over the desert dodging Bedouin camps and Iraqi border patrols.

Though blowing sand obscured the horizon and reduced visibility, the previous weeks' intense training paid off as the helicopters proceeded toward the targets. As the formations approached the drop off point, Pave Lows dropped glowing chemical sticks on the ground to help guide the Apaches. This simple tactic was devised to allow the Apaches to fly over the lights and update their navigation systems before arriving at their targets for the most precise attack possible using their night targeting systems.

The Apache formation made visual contact with the targets (with only one percent moon illumination) 12 kilometers out and achieved target identification at seven kilometers. As they approached the first target, the formation was spotted by an Iraqi sentry who made a run for one of the bunkers. Just as he opened the door, the bunker exploded in a fireball as an AGM-114 Hellfire missile fired from one of the Apaches scored a direct hit.

At 0238 hours the sites were struck simultaneously by Hellfire missiles and Hydra 70 rockets. Both communications vans and the early warning radars were silenced immediately. Almost simultaneously, the second radar station was destroyed. The engagement took place at ranges of three to six kilometers. The mission

The Pave Low can carry any combination of the three machine guns; 7.62mm minigun or the .50 caliber machine gun.

Above:
As a gunner takes aim out the rear ramp, firing the .50 caliber machine gun, the sister ship awaits its turn over target. Note .50 caliber bullet exiting the barrel.

Left:
As the pilots bank sharply during an evasive maneuver, the rear gunner is changing out .50 caliber ammunition. Each gunner wears a safety harness securely fastened to the floor of the helicopter to prevent falling out during just such unexpected maneuvers.

Right:
The venerable .50 caliber machine gun. Though its rate of fire cannot compare with the 7.62 minigun, its range is much greater and the armor-piercing and incendiary rounds are ideal against gun emplacements and personnel carriers.

When not firing the machine guns the gunners keep constant vigil for obstacles and potential threats from their perspective. When a target is identified, the pilots alert the gunners. During the day, the buzz-saw sound of the 7.62mm miniguns is accented by an occasional tracer round. At night, the scene is almost surrealistic as the tracer rounds appear to be a long ribbon of fire snaking its way to the target.

was a total success as both sites were completely destroyed.

En route from the targets, Captain Martin's Pave Low was engaged by two SA-7 missiles — both inside Saudi airspace. Sergeants Berrett Harrison and Terry Null made the calls to break and jettison flares. The jinking helicopter, using infrared counter measures and flares, caused the missiles to miss. Though sobered by the near misses everyone returned safely to base.

Once the air war was underway the Pave Lows became more active in the personnel recovery role. On 19 January 1991 the first recovery opportunity occurred when two MH-53Js were launched out of Rafha to search for a downed F-16 pilot just west of the Talil Airfield. Though the search lasted for over 30 minutes, no direct voice contact was made with the survivor and the rescue attempt was terminated. The mission was significant though, in that to get to the search area the Pave Low helicopters had to fly through dense fog at 100 feet above the desert while evading enemy defenses.

The belief held by Pave Low crews "if we can find them we can get them" was borne out a few days later. The rescue effort occurred on 21 January 1991, and like the earlier efforts, the situation was confusing at first. Initially, word was received that an F-14 and an A-6 had been shot down almost at the same time. Eventually AWACS found out that the A-6 had recovered but that Slate 46 (an F-14 from the USS Saratoga with Lt. Devon Jones and Lt. Larry Slade aboard) had, indeed, been shot down.

Good coordinates were received as well as word that two parachutes had been seen. Plus, it was reported that an A-10 pilot was in voice communication with the downed crew. The AWACS operator who saw the Tomcat disappear

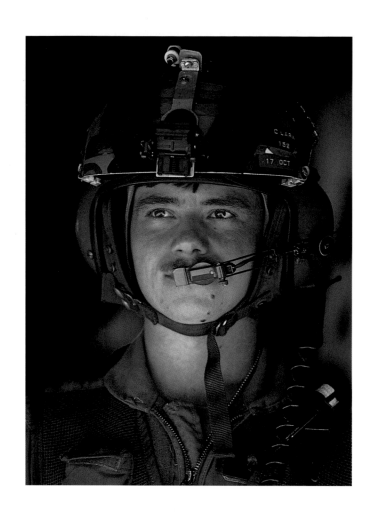

Above:
As the tail gunner fires the .50 caliber, flares can be seen showering down from the aircraft to defeat any missile threats. Pave Low crews frequently dispense M-208 flares on training ranges to ensure that the ALE-40 flare/chaff dispenser works properly and to train crews in system operation.

from his screen located the pilot's position by beacon as being about 50 miles north of Mudaysis Airfield (180 miles into Iraq), about 60 miles north of Baghdad.

MSgt. Tim Hadrych, a gunner aboard an MH-53 (call sign Moccasin 05), recalled "we were pulling alert out of Ar'ar airfield and got a call between 0600 and 0630 that an F-14 was down. They said they had a good location on it and wanted us to get them. We didn't have any time to do in depth mission planning, so we just got up, dressed, and headed for the aircraft."

The weather was absolutely horrible with thick fog. Though visibility approached zero, Captain Tom Trask, pilot of Moccasin 05, and his crew took off as a single ship and, 15 minutes later as copilot Major Mike Homan announced to the crew "we're crossing the fence" (into Iraq), the fog suddenly lifted. As they pressed northward toward the coordinates supplied by AWACS (call sign Yukon) CAP was provided by F-15s. The Pave Low reached the coordinates provided by Yukon and spent the next 20-25 minutes looking for Slate 46 – but to no avail.

In the words of Sergeant Hadrych, "we went to the first search area, flew around and couldn't find anything. As we headed back toward the border we were given another area to search. On the way up we came across some aircraft wreckage, landed and checked it out. It had an ejection seat and a chute but appeared to be of Soviet design . . . it had been there for quite awhile. So we pressed on and still could not find anything in the new search area and could make no voice contact with Alpha or Bravo (the front and back seaters of the downed F-14). While we were out there a couple of Iraqi helicopters tried to converge on us and an enemy Mirage F-1 locked onto us at about eight miles out but our

(DOD photo)

(Photo by Tim Hadrych)

Top:
Two MH-53s refuel at dusk behind an HC-130 Combat Shadow somewhere over the Saudi desert.

Bottom:
The remarkable photo taken by Sgt. Hadrych aboard an MH-53, call sign Moccasin 05, as Navy Lt. Devon Jones is rescued on 21 January, 1991.

Following Pages (100-101):
Rough terrain presents no problem for the big and powerful Pave Low. Note .50 caliber barrel protruding from the right window and the 7.62mm minigun at the left gunner's window.

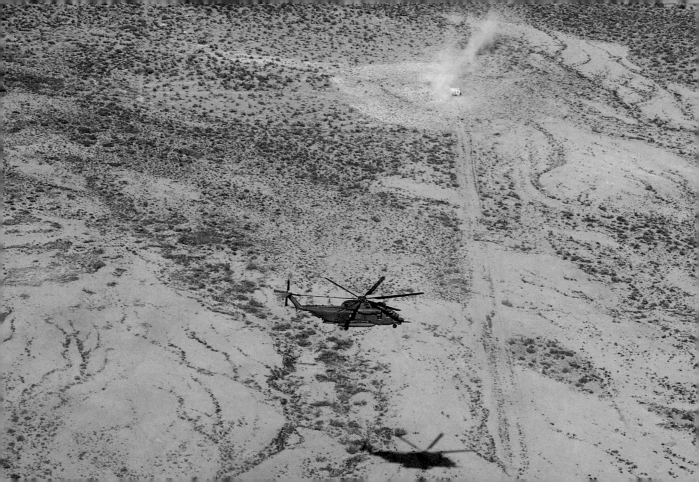

Previous Page:
Left photo shows the Pave Low at its ground hugging best. Photo
on the right shows the accurate firepower of the .50 caliber
machine gun.

fighters chased them off."

The Pave Low was ordered to RTB (return to base) as fuel was getting low and, while in the hot refuel pit, received word from one of the A-10s that voice contact had been established with Lt. Jones. Mocassin 04 and 05 launched at 1220 hours and crossed the border again into Iraq having received good coordinates from the A-10. The A-10s, low on fuel themselves, left the area in search of a tanker.

After flying north for an hour, the Pave Lows came upon the busy Jordan-to-Baghdad highway. Both helicopters stayed south of the highway to avoid detection and waited for a break in the traffic so they could cross over. As Sergeant Hadrych recalls, "the highway was full of traffic. Our sister ship (Mocassin 04) stayed south of the highway as we made a run for it. Our pilot saw an opening and, at only ten feet off the ground, we flew diagonally over the highway at about 140 knots. From there we continued north and flew between two airfields. At one point we were painted by an Iraqi Roland (mobile antiaircraft missile battery). They never fired and we managed to get away."

The other Pave Low remained south of the highway to serve as backup or reinforcements in case they were needed.

The A-10s, back on the scene after refueling, had voice contact with Lt. Jones and joined up with the Pave Low. They told the Pave Low crew that when they flew over Jones' position the lead A-10 would do a vertical pull up maneuver. About 15 minutes after crossing the highway the lead A-10 went vertical and almost immediately the Pave Low made direct voice contact with Lt. Jones. His position was 25 miles north of the first rescue attempt earlier in the day. As the Pave Low began its descent, Sergeant Hadrych, the left door gunner, spotted a truck (assumed to be a radio direction finding unit) headed directly for Jones' position. The helicopter broke to the right in an evasive maneuver as one of the A-10 pilots called out "they're going right at him" to which Major Homan, the Pave Low copilot, replied "smoke the truck!" As the A-10s rolled in, the Pave Low crew could see hits on the truck as it burst into flames.

As the helicopter came back around it headed toward the still smoldering vehicle which was rolling to a stop. The truck was only about 150 yards from where Jones was hiding in a shallow hole he had dug in the desert floor with his bare hands. As the Pave Low touched down, Jones was just off the nose and popped up with a radio in his hand. The two PJs (pararescuemen) aboard the helicopter, Sergeants Tom Bedard and Ben Pennington, exited the aircraft to assist the downed pilot. As one PJ helped Jones aboard, the other provided cover. Once everyone was back on board the Pave Low, the helicopter took off and headed south to join up with their sister ship which had moved north of the highway to be able to react quickly as a cover ship. The A-10s stayed close by in the event they were needed. The flight back to Al Jouf was uneventful and Jones was dropped off at the terminal. It was later learned

AN/APQ-174
Multi-Mode Radar

The Multi-Mode Radar (MMR), a derivative of the very successful AN/APQ-237A LANTIRN terrain following radar, was initially developed for the Bell-Boeing V-22 tilt rotor aircraft. The MMR provides safe, low-level flight down to 100-foot set clearance at night, in adverse weather and in high threat environments.

The MMR incorporates the latest technology and advanced terrain following/terrain avoidance concepts. The radar enables aircraft to perform special operations and search and rescue missions which involve penetrating hostile territory under cover of darkness or adverse weather to deliver (or retrieve) special operations teams or rescue downed air crew and return them to safety.

The MMR is designed for use on a variety of aircraft and has been selected for the Special Operations MH-60K, MH-47E and CV-22.

EXTENDING YOUR REACH
THROUGH SYSTEM SOLUTIONS™

TEXAS INSTRUMENTS

Malcolm Baldrige
National
Quality
Award

1992
Winner

**Defense Systems
& Electronics Group**

Top:
Two MH-53s return to base after a training mission out over the Gulf of Mexico.

Bottom:
On the ramp at Osan AB, Korea, a 31st Special Operations Squadron Pave Low prepares for a mission in a part of the world where tensions run high.

that his backseater, Lt. Slade, had not been as fortunate as he had been captured earlier in the day and made a prisoner of war (and part of the second group of POWs repatriatred at the end of the conflict).

Pave Lows continued personnel recovery alert for the remainder of the war and participated in numerous special forces and Navy SEAL insertion and extraction operations. One such mission included transporting 50 Rangers to the Jordan-Iraq border to destroy a microwave tower.

Following Desert Storm Pave Lows remained active in the region carrying out humanitarian efforts as part of Operation PROVIDE COMFORT in Northern Iraq. They are also involved in and stand ready to assist in NATO's continued involvement in the area around Bosnia.

The MH-53J has been very successful in it's contributions to the United States' defense of freedom throughout the world. The exploits of the aircraft and its flight crews have led to much notoriety. No less important and notable are the efforts of the highly trained and dedicated men and women who maintain these incredibly sophisticated flying machines. To their credit, the MH-53J helicopters were 100 percent mission ready during Operation JUST CAUSE. And, in spite of the harsh desert environment and 125 degree heat, MH-53J maintenance crews had Pave Lows flying within 24 hours of arrival at the Saudi Arabian airport of Dahran. To add to this incredible feat, after five months of desert operations where sand and dust impregnated virtually everything, the MH-53J aircraft carried a 95 percent mission ready rate with 100 percent launch reliability for tasked missions. With their record of accomplishments, flight crews and maintenance personnel proudly stand by their motto "Pave Low leads; anytime, anyplace."

As a Combat Talon lifts off the runway, an all gray MH-53J taxis back to the ramp following a low-level training mission.

Sikorsky Aircraft salutes the men and women of the United States Air Force Air Rescue and Special Operations Forces

UNITED
TECHNOLOGIES
SIKORSKY
AIRCRAFT

Little is known and less has been written about the Night Hawks of the 55th Special Operations Squadron (SOS), 16th Special Operations Wing, based at Hurlburt Field, Florida.

Flying the Sikorsky MH-60G Pave Hawk, the 55th SOS provides long range insertion, extraction and resupply of joint special operations forces as well as augmentation of combat recovery forces.

With the MH-60G Pave Hawk in its

The Sikorsky MH-60G Pave Hawk is a twin-engine medium-lift helicopter optimized for long distance flights over hostile territory at night and in adverse weather. The aircraft has two General Electric T700-GE-700 or T700-GE-701 C engines which give it a tremendous reserve of power. This translates to better maneuverability and better performance in tough environments such as at high density altitudes. The confidence that two engine reliability brings to the crew can't

inventory, the Air Force Special Operations Command can more easily tailor its support to meet the needs of its "customers" which, depending on the mission at hand, include Army Rangers, Navy SEALS, Special Tactics teams and other special forces teams. Due to its small size, reliability, long range and extremely precise navigation, the Pave Hawk is the ideal platform for reconnaissance and surveillance missions where small teams must go long distances to do their work.

be dismissed on an aircraft meant to work deep behind enemy lines. The retractable in-flight refueling probe and a highly accurate, triple redundant navigation system complete the equipement required to make the MH-60G the premier "ride" for the special ops. community.

With a standard flight crew of four; pilot, co-pilot, flight engineer and aerial gunner the Pave Hawk can transport from between eight to 10 fully armed troops, sling load 8,000 pounds of cargo and fight its way into and out of a landing

zone deep behind enemy lines in the dead of night.

With the addition of the External Stores Support Systems (ESSS), the Pave Hawk is capable of carrying an array of armament including two 2.75 inch 19-shot rocket pods, two 20mm cannon pods or two .50 caliber machine

flying at night at low altitude, under constant threat of attack, is an environment with absolutely no margin for error. The Pave Hawk crews epitomize the term "crew concept" as everyone on board takes very seriously the task of calling out terrain, obstacles, location, as well as current and potential threats. Crew coordination and

guns. The standard configuration consists of two side firing crew-served 7.62mm miniguns and up to 2 side-firing .50 caliber machine guns. The flight engineer usually mans the right minigun mounted in the cabin window immediately behind the pilot or the .50 caliber mounted in the right cabin door while the dedicated aerial gunner operates the left minigun mounted in the cabin window behind the co-pilot or the .50 caliber mounted in the right cabin door.

Crews are equipped with night vision goggles (NVG) and maintain coordinated vigilance from their respective positions since

Preceeding page:
An MH-60G hovers as three Army Rangers ascend the ladder. More typically this exercise is conducted at night.

Facing page:
Though the standard armament is either 7.6mm mini-guns or .50 caliber, the M-60G is used in training sorties at Kirtland AFB where MH-60G crews train with the Air Education and Training Command (AETC).

Preceeding Page:
An MH-60G at Kirtland AFB flies low level. The avionics on board the MH-60G allow low level night flying in even featurless terrain.

Above:
The success of any mission depends on the maintenance and support personnel. Maintenance crews are shown conducting preflight checks and routine repairs.

constant communication is essential. Throughout each mission, and especially during night sorties, communications between crew members is an uninterrupted crackle of information concerning landmarks, towers and power lines to be avoided, where the "customers" are, identifying threats and coordinating streams of suppressive machine gun fire to cover the customers as they are dropped off, resupplied or picked up.

The MH-60G Pave Hawk is currently the

transport aircraft.

The Pave Hawk's folding rotor blades and tail stabilator can be quickly positioned, pinned and flight readied shortly after arriving at a forward location via C-5. Up to four fully configured MH-60Gs along with their maintenance package, crews and supplies for 30-days duration can be loaded in one C-5. Transported anywhere in the world, they can be ready for employment in a matter of hours.

only true rapidly deployable, long-range special operations helicopter in the US inventory. While the Army's U/MH-60 Blackhawks are rapidly deployable, operational units currently do not have in-flight refueling capabilities and are thus limited by range even with auxillary fuel tanks. The MH-53J Pave Low, which does have exceptionally long range and is in-flight refuelable, is not as rapidly deployable due to the complexities of reassembly necessitated to accomodate it's bulk within the C-5

Rapid deployment of the Pave Hawk was clearly a factor when the 55th SOS was called to participate in a humanitarian mission to locate the downed aircraft in Ethiopia carrying Congressman Mickey Leland. This was a "no notice" effort which called for four Florida based MH-60Gs, to be air transported by C-5 to Africa.

Although this was a humanitarian rescue mission the rapid deployment scenario was similar to the combat missions for which the 55th constantly trains.

Maintenance crews work around the clock, often in austere conditions to keep the Pave Hawks mission ready.

Left:
Routine hydraulics maintenance.

This page:
Flightline maintenance crews at Hurlburt Field, Fl.

Long before the pilots step to the aircraft, the flight engineers and gunners prepare the Pave Hawk for the mission at hand. The gear is stowed and the pre-flight checks begin. In addition to his other duties the flight engineer also serves as the right door gunner.

Above:
Pave Hawk flight engineer putting 7.62mm ammunition aboard. Note C-5 in background. Four fully equipped Pave Hawks can be transported at one time.

Facing Page and Right:
Pave Hawk gunner reviewing maintenance check list and maintenance write-ups prior to a mission.

Top:
Rope ladder is secured to the floor, orange inflatable raft secured to the bulkhead leaves only enough room for fully equipped special forces "customers".

Middle and bottom:
Supressing gunfire is provided by 7.62mm miniguns (shown) or .50 caliber machine guns.

Above:
The gunner carefully inspects the 7.62mm minigun as part of the pre-mission activities.

Above:
Pave Hawk pilot prepares for a daylight training sortie.

Opposite:
The Pave Hawk is ideally suited for dark, rainy, nighttime missions with its triple redundant navigation system and NVG compatible avionics.

Within 12 hours of their arrival in Ethiopia, Pave Hawk crews were flying ever-expanding search missions supported by HC-130 Combat Shadow refueling aircraft. In spite of poor weather and the needle-in-the-haystack complexity of the mission, the wreckage was located and, though tragically no survivors were found at the wreckage site, the search was concluded in a matter of days.

The ability of Pave Hawk crews to arrive at a specific location at an exact time is essential to the support of special forces teams. The three independent, stand-alone navigation systems on board provide a cross-check capability for extremely precise passive navigation.

The self-contained global positioning system (GPS), doppler and ring laser gyro and inertial navigational systems provide navigation so accurate that standard TACAN guidance is irrelevant. As one senior pilot explains, " . . the Pave Hawk doesn't rely on TACAN for navigation. If someone blows up a TACAN station, or sets another one up as a decoy and you don't know whether you're listening to a real one or not – the Pave Hawk's navigation system permits us to arrive at a specific location at an exact time".

The MH-60G Pave Hawk utilizes an automatic flight control system and a fully automatic forward looking infrared (FLIR) slued to flight path vector enabling the crew to follow terrain contours and avoid obstacles at night.

The 55th SOS, as with every other special operations squadron in the 16th Special Operations Wing (SOW), train in as realistic an environment as possible working closely with its customers. Or as a commanding officer aptly puts it "if you're not training jointly . . . you're not training!". The squadron's training is intense. It routinely includes a combination of low-level precision navigation at night using night vision goggles, NVG shipboard operations and aerial

*Air refueling is up close and personal. As an
HC-130N, Combat Shadow flies straight and level
the pilot of the Pave Hawk flies to the refueling
basket. The extendable refueling probe provides the
clearance necessary to keep the refueling hose from
the tanker away from the helicopter's rotor. In
actual operations this same scene is accomplished
at night aided by night vision goggles.*

refueling, a variety of alternate personnel insertion/extraction methods over land and water, and cargo sling operations all performed over various terrain and in a wide spectrum of conditions to include desert, arctic, tropical and mountain locations worldwide.

The realism of the squadron's training has paid huge dividends in actual combat. During Operation JUST CAUSE, the 55th SOS demonstrated its capabilities by performing numerous combat recovery missions. In the opening phase of Just Cause a blocking force of Army Rangers, who had been left on the ground, were picked up and taken back to Howard AFB.

In the predawn hours of December 20, 1989, the squadron was called upon to support Navy SEALS pinned down at Paitilla Airport in downtown Panama City. A pilot involved with the mission recalled "... the airstrip was one of the spots where they thought Noriega might try to escape. The SEALS met some pretty fierce resistance there and, unfortunately, three SEALS were killed. They needed immediate reinforcement, so one of our Hawks and a Pave Low were tasked to do that. We went up to Rodman Naval Air Station, which is just up the canal from Howard AFB, picked up a group of SEALS for reinforcement, and flew them into Paitilla, which was hot at the time. Shooting was still going on between the SEALS and the Panama Defense Forces (PDF).

"With the Pave Low flying cover we went in, dropped off our reinforcements, picked up the bodies of the three SEALS, took off and circled overhead as the Pave Low went in and dropped off its reinforcements. As we headed in and out of Howard AFB, we were repeatedly fired on from the Bridge of Americas. Though we were not hit it was a unique situation to see tracers coming right at your helicopter. As a result of the intense fire fights on the ground in the first 24 hours of fighting, we air evacuated 18 guys back to Howard . . . wounded Rangers, SEALS and Special Forces troops". The firepower of the MH-60G's M-60D machine gun also made quite an impression on the Panamanians. Captured PDF troops often referred to the "Black Hawk with the cannon" confusing the refueling probe for a cannon, such was the volume of fire the Pave Hawk's guns put out.

With its inflight refueling capabilities, the
Pave Hawk's range is limited only by aircrew
endurance.

Above:
Pilots begin the approach to the HC-130N Combat
Shadow tanker. The tanker is visible in the
center section of the windscreen.

Below:
The Pave Hawk pilot's view of the Combat Shadow
during refueling.

During DESERT STORM the Pave Hawk crews again supported Special Forces teams while working in concert with the MH-53J Pave Lows of the 20th SOS. For most of the crews Desert Storm was their first taste of combat. As one gunner recalls "you can't really describe the feeling. You've been training for this type of situation and when it happens – you just do it. Just like in the States only this time the shooting is both ways and for real. During DESERT STORM I was assigned to the recovery task force for the initial hit on the early warning radar sites in Western Iraq. I thought 'this is the big one'. We planned our route and checked the threats and went into crew rest. That evening you could tell everyone was a little nervous, but we had a mission to do. As we orbited over the hold point between the two radar sites, all we could do was wait. As the two groups of Apaches led by the Pave Lows crossed the border at "H" hour, first the western radar site was taken out, a couple of seconds later the eastern site was under attack. AAA was shooting up into the sky for about a minute. The rest of the night was something else, watching the explosions in the north (Western Iraq) and waiting to be called in."

(DOD photo)

(DOD Photo)

Facing Page:
MH-60G in its distinctive "flare" before landing where the tail wheel touches down first.

This Page:
Pave Hawks in Saudi during DESERT STORM.

(DOD Photo)

Ruggedly reliable, the Pave Hawk can assist waterborn Special Forces teams with offshore insertion and extractions.

The Pave Hawks, teamed with the MH-53J Pave Lows were split into two groups; one working in the western part of Iraq and the other near the Kuwait-Saudi border near where the battle of Khafji was fought. During the war, the 55th's Pave Hawks were on call for special forces teams to provide fire support and recovery in the event they were compromised.

Pave Hawks were also responsible for combat recovery of Coalition air forces from five miles off the coast of Kuwait to 10 miles out and beyond.

Once the ground war began and the push was made to liberate Kuwait City, Pave Hawk crews were involved with infiltrating special forces teams to the US Embassy and supported the efforts to secure the airport.

The sturdiness and precision of the MH-60G Pave Hawk combined with the superior training and dedication of the members of the 55th Special Operations Squadron can best be summarized in the words of one of the pilots "I

At left an impromptu meeting between a Pave Hawk pilot and an Army Ranger team.

Above:
A 55th SOS Pave Hawk pops over a tree line to insert a Ranger team at a pre-determined landing zone.

Following Pages:
As a 55th SOS Pave Hawk settles to about 30' off the ground, Army Rangers climb aboard by way of a rope ladder. Note gunner assisting the Rangers aboard.

Above:
A 3-man Army Ranger team in a non-typical serene setting sans gear. Rangers and other special forces teams routinely train with the 55th SOS to perfect their techniques of behind enemy lines warfare.

Facing Page:
Army Rangers using the Fast rope as the Pave Low pilots hover a landing zone.

flew my first combat mission over Iraq from Incirlik Air Base, Turkey. It was a no-notice launch to recover a downed pilot. I was very excited at the thought of going into hostile territory and performing exactly the type of mission for which I had trained for so long. At the same time, I was mindful of the fact I might not come back. By this I do not mean I was hesitant to go, only respectful of the risks involved. In the objective area we took fire several times and I remember my reaction being one of anger at the faceless foe shooting at us. We made it back safely, however, due to our outstanding training and remarkably capable aircraft. The MH-60G Pave Hawk is a wonderful combat helicopter – reliable, rugged, maneuverable – and a joy to fly".

Regardless of where the call may come, anywhere in the world, in daylight or dark or adverse weather, Special Forces teams know that the 55th Special Operations Squadron is prepared and ready to respond. With their highly trained and dedicated crews flying the reliable and rapidly deployable MH-60G Pave Hawks, the 55th SOS makes good the claim of their motto "Always Ready. Always There".

SPECIAL TACTICS

The 720th Special Tactics Group, home-based at Hurlburt Field, FL, is the functional manager for special tactics squadrons worldwide. There are a total of 4 squadrons, 2 based in the Continental United States (CONUS) and one in each of the two major overseas theaters in Europe and the Pacific (SOCEUR and SOCPAC). The 720 STG organizes, trains, and equips special tactics Combat Control Teams (CCTs) and Pararescuemen (PJs) personnel for deployment anywhere in the world in support of USSOCOM activities.

CCTs and PJs are usually the first AFSOC personnel inserted into a hostile area and almost always the last ones out. Highly trained and motivated special tactics teams provide quick reaction command and control, positive air traffic management, and casualty recovery, treatment and evacuation staging during joint air and ground/maritime operations. The combat controllers are air traffic controllers specialized in control of austere assault zone operations. They perform a number of time critical tasks including the establishment of landing zones, setting up navigational aids, ensuring communication links with air assault aircraft and providing guidance for strike aircraft and naval gunfire. Special Tactics Pararescuemen are skilled in advanced emergency medical trauma treatment. They provide emergency trauma care for the wounded, mass casualty triage and establish collection and transfer points for the wounded. As the first AFSOC forces on the ground at an objective, the synergy of the two unique capabilities ensure the success of their mission.

Below:
Special Tactics personnel insert by parachute using static line or military free fall techniques.

Facing Page:
As a Combat Controller communicates with arriving aircraft a PJ keeps a vigil for any enemy troops.

The concept of employing advance forces on the ground to help guide air assault forces to their drop zones originated in World War II. As a result of problems encountered during airborne operations in Sicily, Italy, at Normandy and in Holland, special pathfinder units were created. They were trained and equipped to spearhead the main assault force to provide weather, enemy strength and navigational information.

These special pathfinder units evolved into the modern day CCTs. Pararescue came about as a result of concerns over the haphazard conduct of rescue operations during WWII. Once the Air Rescue Service was established in 1946, a need for a skilled medical ground force became evident. Borrowing a concept from U.S. Forest Service smoke jumpers, the rescue jumper concept matured to pararescue teams and fulfilled the need for highly specialized medical technicians.

Since the emergence of the Air Force as a separate service, Combat Controllers and Pararescuemen have been involved in practically every international crisis where U.S. forces have been involved. They have also provided humanitarian assistance in response to natural disasters throughout the world.

The first major use of the special tactics concept occurred during Operation EAGLE CLAW/RICE BOWL when special tactics teams established the refueling site for Desert One.

During Operation URGENT FURY in Grenada and JUST CAUSE in Panama CCTs and PJs worked closely with their Army and Navy counterparts to provide recon and landing zone surveillance, air traffic control and emergency trauma care.

In Operation DESERT STORM, Special Tactics Teams, working out of forward operating locations (FOLs) provided a ready pool of assets for various missions. The PJs often served as medical crewmen aboard MH-53s, MH-60s, CH-47s, and UH-60s. Combat controllers went into Rafha Airfield to help marshal the flow of aircraft moving the 18th Airborne Corps and the 82nd Airborne Division into position. At Al Jouf and Ar'ar airfields CCTs operated the Forward Area Refueling and Rearming Points (FARRPs) refueling hundreds of aircraft either battle damaged or at "minimum fuel". They also provided airfield management services until relieved by much larger support units. They then redeployed to forward areas to place strike and navigation beacons along the northern Saudi border to help update the navigation systems for aircraft flying to targets in Iraq.

Late in January 1991, a special unit of Coalition Forces, including a combat controller, infiltrated within 15 kilometers of Baghdad on a classified mission to provide close air support (CAS) communication. The Combat Controller's knowledge of CAS activities was so impressive and the mission so successful that other special tactics personnel accompanied similar deep penetration missions.

Special Tactics Combat Controllers and Pararescuemen are continually training on their insertion and extraction techniques to include HALO (high-altitude, low-opening), HAHO (high-altitude, high-opening) and static line jumping, soft boat and hard boat work, helicopter deployments both over water and land, and off-road and all-terrain vehicle operations. CCT and PJ personnel are also expertly trained in weapons proficiency, SCUBA, communications, and field navigation.

A little known fact and yet one of the best testimonials to the special tactics concept occurred late in February 1991. It was a special tactics team that opened Kuwait International Airport to Coalition Air Forces. Pararescuemen helped clear the runway while Combat Controllers set up radio communications and portable NAVAIDS.

On yet another mission, this time to Kuwait City, a four-man special tactics team fast-roped from two MH-53 and two Army MH-60 helicopters onto a 15-story building. From their vantage point they were able to provide command and control communications in support of Coalition aircraft.

As the ground war began several special tactics pararescuemen served as front line combat medics while others flew aeromedical evacuation missions.

Combat Controllers and Pararescuemen are often at the very forefront of hostile action. Their ability to sort out mission priorities and act decisively amidst the "fog of war" is often the difference between life and death. The professionalism, personal commitment and skill exemplified by special tactics personnel was dramatically demonstrated in Somalia on the 3rd and 4th of October 1993 when a U.S. UH-60 helicopter was shot down by a rocket propelled grenade. In what turned out to be the longest, most vicious fire fight since Vietnam, several special tactics personnel distinguished themselves during the rescue attempt.

Technical Sergeant Timothy A. Wilkinson, a U.S. Air Force Pararescueman with the 24th

Above:
Combat Controllers provide critical "eyes on" an objective via long haul communications using LST-5 SATCOM and PRC 104 HF radios.

Below:
A 4-wheel Quad used to infiltrate in rough terrain.

Facing Page:
Combat Controllers use a variety of radios that allow communication with arriving aircraft by line-of-sight or around the globe on SATCOM and/or HF.

STSQ, made a fast rope insertion and was met by intense small arms and RPG fire from three directions. As they reached the crash site, Sergeant Wilkinson's team set up a casualty collection point. Under continuous fire Sergeant Wilkinson made his way to the downed helicopter and provided trauma care to an injured crew chief and helped evacuate him to the relative safety of the casualty collection point. Remaining in the wreckage trying to assist a second trapped crewman, Sergeant Wilkinson was wounded in the face and arm as bullets and shrapnel slammed into the helicopter. Despite his wounds he was able to free the injured crew chief, stabilize his condition and evacuate him. The sergeant then noticed that a Ranger security element was under fire across a four-way intersection and had taken casualties. He broke cover and raced through a barrage of small arms fire where he treated three seriously wounded Rangers. After his supply of medical supplies was exhausted he again crossed the fire swept intersection to the helicopter, retrieved additional medical supplies and returned to the wounded Rangers where he provided treatment until their evacuation the next morning.

During the same operation, Special Tactics Combat Controller, Staff Sergeant Jeffrey W. Bray, directed supporting fire from overhead helicopter gunships. He developed an ingenious perimeter marking system and called in deadly fire support against concealed targets – many less than 15 meters away. Eye witnesses testified that his courage and coolness under accurate and intense

fire while directing precise helicopter gunfire kept a determined enemy from overrunning the team.

Also on the scene to assist the downed Blackhawk crew was Master Sergeant Scott C. Fales, a 24th Special Tactics Squadron Pararescueman. While conducting an initial assessment at the crash site, Sergeant Fales was shot and seriously wounded in the leg. Despite his painful wound, he took care of the other members of his CSAR team who had also been wounded. At one point in the fire fight Sergeant Fales shouted a warning as several enemy hand grenades were thrown near their make-shift defensive position and shielded the injured with his own body. Throughout the fire fight he not only provided expert trauma care for the wounded but provided covering fire against repeated enemy attacks.

For extraordinary heroism, TSgt. Wilkinson was awarded the Air Force Cross, and the Silver Star for Gallantry was awarded to MSgt. Fales and SSgt. Bray. Additionally, special tactics personnel earned Four Bronze Stars with Valor, Four Bronze Stars and four Purple Hearts.

When AC-130s were called on to support UNISOM forces in Mogadishu, 720 STG Combat Controllers provided critical C^2 and terminal guidance for every round fired.

The discipline to perform their duty and to provide expert care and support in such hellish conditions is a tribute to the training and commitment of every Special Tactics Team member.

Following Page:
Special Tactics "RAMZ" (Rigging Alternate Method Zodiac) rubber boat raiding craft airdrop over water. Note fins on jumpers.

Facing Page and Below:
Pararescuemen (PJ) are often the first on the scene. They are able to provide emergency trauma care during the quickly changing dynamics of combat, stabilizing the wounded and coordinating their evacuation.

155

THERE IS
NO SUCH THING
AS LOW INTENSITY
CONFLICT....

WHEN
THEY ARE
SHOOTING AT YOU!

The proven leader in
electronic countermeasures systems,
sophisticated simulators and
combat systems.

TRACOR

6500 Tracor Lane
Austin, Texas 78725-2000
Phone: (512) 926-2800
FAX: (512) 929-2241

The AC-130U is scheduled to enter service in late 1994 and will feature improved avionics and an all-weather attack radar.

Of all the AFSOC assets, perhaps the Spectre gunship has received the most notoriety. Gunship crews have demonstrated in Grenada, Panama, Iraq, Kuwait and Somalia the importance of precision close air support.

The AC-130 Spectre gunship is an extensively modified version of the Lockheed C-130. The Spectre first saw action in 1968 during the Southeast Asia conflict. While its primary missions are close air support, air interdiction, and armed reconnaissance, it also provides perimeter and point defense, armed escort, landing zone support, forward air control, limited command, control, and communications (C^3) and combat search and rescue.

AFSOC has at its disposal two versions of the gunship; the AC-130H flown by the 16th Special Operations Squadron, located at Hurlburt Field, FL and the older AC-130A flown by the Air Force Reserve's 711th Special Operations Squadron of the 919th Special Operations Wing based at Duke Field, FL.

The AC-130H is armed with two 20mm Vulcan cannons set to fire 2500 rounds per minute each, one 40mm Bofors cannon set to fire at 100 rounds per minute and one 105mm Howitzer able to fire as fast as it can be loaded; about eight rounds per minute. The "A" model carries two 20mm cannons, two 40mm Bofors cannons and two 7.62mm miniguns.

The "H" model is air refuelable and can loiter on station almost indefinitely with tanker support while the "A" model is not air refuelable.

The latest version of the gunship, the AC-130U is scheduled to enter service in late 1994. Thirteen aircraft are on order and as they are delivered to the 16th SOS, the eight "H" models will be transferred to the Air Force Reserve 711th SOS, significantly enhancing their capabilities. The ten "A" models will be retired from service.

AC-130 SPECTRE GUNSHIP

In addition to an improved avionics suite, 360 degree field of view infrared and all-light level television sensors, the "U" model will have a true all-weather capability with an attack radar similar to the one used in the F-15E Strike Eagle. The weapon configuration will differ somewhat in that the AC-130U will have one trainable 25mm Gatling gun replacing the two fixed 20mm cannons. The 25mm cannon will give the Spectre increased standoff range and improve survivability. The 40mm and 105mm cannon will be retained in the current configuration.

The AC-130 features an integrated sensor suite consisting of an all-light level television sensor and an infrared sensor. Radar and electronic sensors also give the gunship a method of positively identifying friendly ground forces while delivering ordnance at night and in adverse weather. Navigational equipment includes the inertial navigation system (INS) and global positioning system (GPS) allowing the gunship to position itself with an accuracy measured in dozens of feet.

The AC-130 Spectre gunship is normally crewed by two pilots, navigator (NAV), fire control officer (FCO), electronic warfare officer (EWO), flight engineer (FE), infrared (IR) sensor and low-light level television (LTV) sensor operators, five gunners, and a loadmaster (LM).

Crew coordination is an essential part of the gunship mission. The pilots fly the airplane with the aircraft commander actually firing the weapons; the navigator directs the flight to and from the target; the flight engineer makes sure all the aircraft systems are operating smoothly; the sensor operators identify and pinpoint targets using the sensors with the best picture; the fire control officer relays target information, weapon and ammunition selection to the pilot; the electronics warfare officer (EWO) is responsible for threat detection and threat avoidance; the gunners load and maintain the weapons, and the loadmaster keeps constant vigil out the tail for any potential threats. A gunner also pulls right scanner and flight deck or hatch-bubble scanner duties.

While the gunship concept can be traced to WWII, during Vietnam the AC-47 "Puff/Spooky", AC-119 "Shadow/Stinger" and the "A" and "H" model AC-130s destroyed more than 10,000 enemy vehicles and were credited with many life-saving close air support missions.

The first trial by fire since Vietnam occurred when gunships from Hurlburt Field departed on the evening of 24 October, 1983, to participate in Operation URGENT FURY. The all night flight from Florida to Grenada took almost ten hours and required two heavyweight inflight refuelings.

Captain Mike Couvions and his gunship crew arrived over Port Salines on 25 October and, while performing area reconnaissance, noticed that the airfield was littered with telephone poles, trucks and other obstructions. The information was radioed back to headquarters where plans were changed to air drop the ground forces rather than attempt landings on the obstacle strewn airfield.

Too often in recounting the exploits of aircrew members the maintenance and support personnel are overlooked. Any aircrew member will tell you how important the behind the scenes efforts of the combat support, medical, communications and security personnel are. Everyone involved has a key role. Any accomplishment achieved by the aircrew is a direct tribute to the quality of hard work and dedication of the maintenance and support crews on the ground. The fact that gunship aircrews were able to reliably execute combat missions – sometimes in aircraft over 35 years old – is evidence of the hard work by everyone involved.

Lt. Colonel David V. Simms, 16th SOS Director of Operations at the time of URGENT FURY, and his crew along with Major Clement W. Twiford's crew were scheduled to depart Hurlburt at two minute intervals. LtC. Simms' aircraft, however, blew an engine shortly after takeoff and orbited the field until enough fuel had been burned off to attempt an emergency landing. After safely landing the crippled aircraft, LtC. Simms and his crew transferred to a spare gunship and pressed on with their mission to Grenada.

After flying all night, Major Twiford's crew arrived over Point Salines airfield just before dawn. As Chief Master Sergeant Michael Hosenbackez recalled, "It was still dark when we arrived over the airfield. The enemy could hear us but apparently could not see us as they were probing the sky with searchlights trying to find us. We remained overhead until daylight when, at the first light of day, the enemy gunners finally saw us. That's when the antiaircraft artillery (AAA) started spitting." Major Twiford's crew called the command center and told them they were receiving heavy AAA and were going "HOT" (arming the weapons in preparation for an attack). Just as the crew engaged the antiaircraft sites, the gunship's firing mechanism malfunctioned and the gunners had to manually fire the 105mm howitzer. As the fire control officer directed the gunfire, the gunners used the hand-pulled lanyard to fire the weapon. Despite the problem, the gunship crew was able to put down an accurate barrage of cannon fire.

As Major Twiford's gunship orbited above the airfield, the crew received an urgent request for fire support from friendly forces on the ground. "We were engaging the antiaircraft sites," noted CMSgt. Hosenbackez, "when Major Twiford received a call from our troops on the ground saying they were pinned down under a truck and needed our help. Major Twiford told them to dig in and they responded by saying they were already dug in. We started putting down 105mm howitzer fire into a house on a hill occupied by the enemy. We had to fire several rounds of 105mm to stop the enemy because they were down in the basement firing at our ground forces." Major Twiford's crew also silenced five ZU-23-2 AAA sites plus numerous heavy machine gun and mortar positions with their 20mm, 40mm, and 105mm cannon fire. Low on fuel and completely out of ammunition, Major Twiford's crew finally called it a day after nearly 17 hours in the air. For their efforts over Grenada to help rescue American students, the crew received the General William H. Turner award as the Outstanding Aircrew in Military Airlift Command (MAC).

Maintenance crew working on the beacon tracking radar. Note proximity of 40mm cannon.

PHANTOM OF THE OPS.

In any theater, ITT's AN/ALQ-172 ECM System delivers an outstanding performance.

LtC. Simms' gunship, call sign Lima 57, finally entered the fight over Grenada and immediately responded to calls for fire support. In spite of heavy AAA fire, LtC. Simms' gunship destroyed five enemy buildings and a manned bunker near the airfield where several fires and secondary explosions were observed following their attack. The crew also provided vectors for a U.S. Navy helicopter as it searched for a downed U.S. Army helicopter three miles east of the airfield. As the gunship provided aircover over the crash site, multiple rescue flights evacuated the wounded helicopter crewmembers and passengers.

After a quick side trip to Barbados to reload and rearm, LtC. Simms' crew returned to the fray and halted enemy advances on friendly positions with highly accurate 20mm cannon fire and silenced two antiaircraft sites with their 105mm. Responding to an urgent call for assistance, LtC. Simms' crew destroyed three enemy armored personnel carriers (APCs)

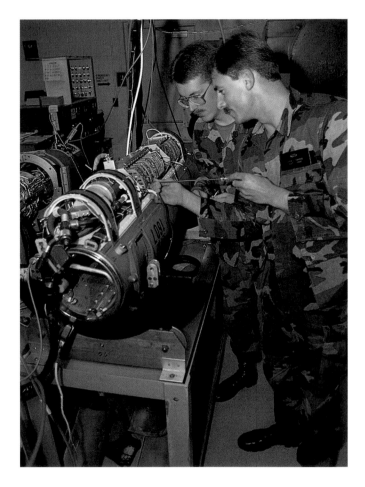

Heavily armed, the AC-130 uses sophisticated sensor, navigation and fire control systems integrated with a lethal array of side-firing weapons to provide surgical firepower or area saturation during extended loiter periods, at night and in adverse weather.

advancing on a parked C-141. All three enemy vehicles were destroyed when the gunship crew fired four rounds of 105mm.

The gunship mission is to provide precision, close air support in a closely defined mission profile. As one Spectre pilot states, "if you just need something destroyed, there are other airplanes with bigger punch that move a lot faster and can even deliver precision weapons at night. But if you have somebody on the ground who needs fire support close to his position . . . then that is where the gunship really performs a special mission."

Operation JUST CAUSE in Panama provided further proof of the gunship's effectiveness. Though JUST CAUSE was quickly concluded, several active duty and reserve gunship crews gained recognition for distinguished action. It was also the baptism of fire for the new multi-ship tactic "Top-Hat". Only thirty days prior to JUST CAUSE, Major Emmett "Otis" Redding developed the multi-ship "Top-Hat" tactic where two gunships working the same area flew concentric orbits. One crew from the 1st Special Operations Wing, commanded by Captain Francis R. Gabreski (son of the famed

Facing Page: Flightline crews seek shelter from the sun in the shadow of the gunship. Note scanners bubble. While on combat missions the scanner keeps watch for any missile or AAA threats.

This Page: Flightline maintenance is performed round the clock to keep the gunship mission ready.

WWII ace) performed an almost textbook example of what the Spectre could do when used in multi-ship ground support missions. He was only the third pilot trained in the "Top-Hat" tactic.

On 20 December 1989, Captain Gabreski's crew made a heavyweight takeoff from Hurlburt Field, Florida into poor weather conditions. After quickly boresighting the weapons in the Gulf of Mexico they joined a five-ship formation of gunships led by 16th SOS Director of Operations Lt. Colonel Mike Guidry and crew. The long flight to Panama involved flying low-level over the water to evade early warning radar and two night-time in-flight refuelings. The crew was assigned a close air support and armed reconnaissance mission in conjunction with a U.S. Army Special Forces team trying to secure the Rio Pacora Bridge. The objective was to prevent Panamanian Defense Forces (PDF) from reinforcing Torrijos/Tocumen Airport and Panama City. After the eight hour flight from Hurlburt, the gunship arrived on the scene about the same time as the Army Special Forces ground team and responded immediately to the call to stop a column of five enemy vehicles moving towards the bridge from Fort Cimarron. The gunship rolled in overhead laying down an explosive barrage of highly accurate 40mm and 105mm rounds. The leading vehicle, a troop-laden personnel carrier, received a direct hit which effectively halted the convoy. Several other vehicles were observed heading toward friendly positions and, likewise, were destroyed or halted by the gunship's intense and accurate cannon fire. The PDF battalion, despite heavy losses, continued their attack across the bridge on foot. In spite of small arms and heavy machine gun fire, Captain Gabreski's crew brought their 20mm cannons to bear and halted the enemy advance – sometimes having to fire within 80 meters of the friendly position. In three separate instances, enemy forces tried to cross the bridge only to be repulsed each time by the gunship's concentrated firepower. After the attackers were repelled for the final time, the gunship provided armed reconnaissance in the area for the remainder of the night. Captain Gabreski and his crew destroyed nine vehicles and inflicted heavy casualties to the enemy force and were instrumental in preventing any friendly casualties. For this action, Captain Gabreski was awarded the James Jabara Award for Airmanship.

Another "Top-Hat" mission was flown by 1st SOW Spectre crews further highlighting the gunship's capabilities during the night of 20 December 1989. Captain Charles G. McMillan's crew and Captain James Hughes' crew were part

of a two-gunship formation that attacked the PDF headquarters compound, La Comandancia. Captain McMillan's crew, as stated in their Mackay Trophy recommendation, "significantly reduced the number of American casualties and ensured the successful occupation of key military positions." Specifically, Captain McMillan and his crew adjusted to several last minute target changes in a very complex mission, including a

headquarters compound was virtually obliterated while adjacent structures received little or no damage at all." With the destruction of the compound, the single highest-valued target during JUST CAUSE, PDF personnel were dispersed, command and control was severed and enemy troops were generally demoralized. The gunship crews continued their barrage of 40mm cannon fire destroying two separate PDF positions

The AC-130H carries two types of counter measure jamming pods. Shown here is the QRC-84-02A. Not shown is the QRC-80-01.

critical time-over-target (TOT) of plus or minus seven seconds, and rolled in over La Comandancia exactly on time. Despite AAA fire, which brought down a U.S. Army aircraft, the two gunships took out six specific targets in less than five minutes. Even though the compound was situated in a heavily populated area, post battle surveys by U.S. Army personnel certified that "the

reportedly firing rocket propelled grenades at U.S. soldiers only 20 meters away. Their attack silenced the opposition, prevented reinforcement, and allowed U.S. forces to advance and hold positions on the main street in front of the La Comandancia. The gunships remained over the headquarters facilities providing further support for Army personnel operating both inside and outside the compound, destroying four .50 caliber

Threat Avoidance

Watkins-Johnson ESM systems ensure mission effectiveness through early detection of the electronic threat.

Prepare for tomorrow's
mission today . . .

*Specify
W-J*

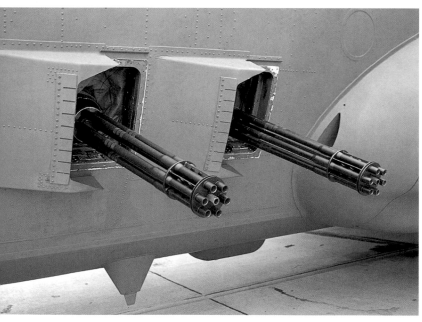

Previous Page:
Munitions handling specialists in the hot cargo area push cart loaded with 105mm, 40mm and 20mm ammunition. The pilots shut down the two right engines while ammo is being loaded.

Facing Page:
Top left: 40mm ammunition being loaded. Top right: Gunner loads 20mm through right observation window.

Bottom Left:
20mm Vulcan cannons.

Bottom Right:
Munitions handling specialists loading 40mm ammunition.

This Page:
After all ammunition is loaded gunners and munitions handling specialists push ammo cart away from the aircraft.

machine guns. In spite of dense smoke and flames caused by secondary explosions, the crews were further credited with the destruction of an enemy mortar position. When U.S. Army personnel inside the PDF compound received fire from the main headquarters building, they sought gunship assistance in spite of the close proximity of their own personnel. Captain Hughes' crew quickly fired numerous rounds of 105mm into the target without a single miss. Within minutes, the sniper's sanctuary had been reduced to burned-out rubble. After U.S. forces gained control of the PDF headquarters, Captain Hughes and his crew were released to support U.S. Marine forces heavily engaged by PDF personnel at Fort Amador. Operating with limited information, in the middle of the night, the gunship crew quickly identified the exact location of the U.S. forces and provided air support. After this engagement, Captain Hughes' gunship departed the area to rendezvous with a tanker. However, before the aerial refueling began the crew was informed of a renewed attack on the Marine position. Although their aircraft was

Gunners and munitions handling specialists load the AC-130H at the hot cargo area. The gunship carries 100 rounds of 105mm, 256 rounds of 40mm and 3,000 rounds of 20mm ammunition.

Top:
Munitions handling specialists at the hot cargo area as gunship is being loaded with live ammunition. Note two right engines are shut down while left engines remain running.

Lower Right:
Loadmaster takes a final walk around before take-off.

almost out of fuel, they returned to Ft. Amador, located the friendly position on the ground, targeted the PDF forces, and repelled the attack. They then accomplished a successful aerial refueling and were directed to yet another mission. There, the crew provided support for ground units and relayed valuable situation updates to various command and control centers. Finally, after 10 hours of flying, including combat, the gunships landed safely at Howard Air Force Base.

The gunship mission over La Comandancia was unique as it was the first time in combat that one gunship flew a concentric orbit above another. At times, the aircraft at higher altitude

AC-130H gunship taxis from hot cargo area with a full load of ammunition.

had to fire within 50 feet of the other aircraft. It was also the first time in combat that gunship crews used night-vision goggles (NVG).

The tenacity, skill and courage of the AC-130 gunship crews was further exemplified by a crew initially tasked to provide support at Rio Hato Air Base. After leaving Hurlburt and an eight hour flight to Panama, Captain Mark Transue and his crew rolled in on their target and encountered heavy AAA fire from every section of the air base. The crew engaged the gun positions knowing they had less than two minutes to silence AAA fire before U.S. C-130s carrying over 500 airborne Rangers and numerous equipment pallets were to be airdropped. The infrared sensor operator, MSgt. Fred Kramer located the first target, a stationary ZPU-4 AAA weapon, and it was destroyed with the 105mm howitzer. The gunship continued to encounter AAA fire from two armored personnel carriers. Switching to the rapid-fire mode, the crew destroyed both targets in quick succession and destroyed three moving targets and other stationary AAA sites as the troop

laden C-130s approached the airfield. Captain Transue was soon contacted by the Rangers on the ground and started working calls for fire support with troops-in-contact. Following these attacks, the Ranger forces were able to secure the airfield and establish a strong defensive position. For the next five hours the gunship fired on targets around the airfield in near-perfect coordination with friendly forces on the ground destroying enemy antiaircraft positions and pockets of resistance.

Captain Transue and his crew finally landed at Howard Air Force Base after logging almost 16 hours in the air – of which eight hours were spent in grueling close air support.

The involvement of the Air Force Reserve 919th Special Operations Group (SOG) based at Duke Field, FL was a case of being in the right place and the right time. Earlier in the month, two aircraft of the 711th Special Operations Squadron were dispatched to Howard Air Force Base to conduct joint training exercises with U.S. Army and Marine ground personnel and to provide security augmentation to forces guarding United States facilities in Panama.

As the situation between the United States and the Noriega regime worsened, the 919th SOG was placed on 24-hour alert. Training flights continued as did the exercises with the Marine, Army and Navy SEAL forces. Reconnaissance missions were also conducted to provide intelligence updates on the Panama Defense Force Comandancia, Toboga Island, the Bamboa Prison and other areas in and around Panama City. At the time, the 919th SOG operated the only AC-130 gunships in Panama prior to Operation JUST CAUSE. The unit assumed the responsibility for all gunship activity until the active duty aircraft arrived on station at 2300 hours on 18 December.

Although the Air Force Reserve crews were not involved in the invasion planning or, for that matter, even considered in any of the operational plans or rehearsal missions, they were notified on 19 December that their services were needed in a "shooting war". The two AC-130A crews quickly assembled all available intelligence data, developed and briefed a plan of action for their own involvement. They were finally briefed on the JUST CAUSE plan only six hours before H-hour and assigned air base defense for Howard Air Force Base.

Initially scrambled at 2219 hours on 19 December, aircraft "Proud Warrior" piloted by Majors Clay McCutchan and Mike Milton became the first gunship airborne from Howard AFB for Operation JUST CAUSE.

After sensor alignment and reconnaissance of the base perimeter the aircraft was ordered to return to Howard AFB and resume alert status. The crew was launched from alert status on its second mission at 0035 hours on 20 December 1989, in response to a reported attack on the main gate of Howard by PDF forces. After a thorough search of the area the crew was

Flight Deck Crew

Facing Page:
As pilot banks the aircraft to the distinctive 30° bank and lines up the target on the HUD the co-pilot keeps a close watch on the flight instruments.

Top:
As pilot plots firing pass by peering through the HUD, other flight deck crew look on.

Bottom:
Navigator is seated on the left and to his right is the fire control officer (FCO).

Puffs of smoke from the 20mm Vulcan cannons can be seen as an AC-130H begins its firing pass.

unable to locate the enemy and resumed their mission of airbase defense. By this time close air support requests were coming from almost every agency involved in the conflict. Major McCutchan's aircraft was diverted to search for an Army helicopter reportedly down in the waterway of the Panama Canal. While searching the area, the crew was again diverted to support ground forces under fire on Albrook AFS. After contacting the ground forces and locating several targets, the crew fired on four targets as directed by the forward air controller (FAC). The gunship headed home to Howard only to be diverted again to locate and destroy three armored personnel carriers reportedly headed toward U.S. forces. The vehicles were declared hostile by the Air Operations Center and the crew was given clearance to fire. As the pilots maneuvered the aircraft for a firing pass on the vehicles, the Fire

Facing Page

Top Right:
AC-130H electronic warfare officer (EWO).

Bottom Right:
AC-130H low-light level television operator.

Control Officer Major James N. Strength, attempted to locate any friendly forces in the area. Seeking further clarification from the Air Operations Center, the gunship was given the go ahead to fire on the vehicles when, at the last minute, television sensor operator Master Sergeant Walter L. Watley noticed what appeared to be friendly troops among the vehicles and informed Major Strength who advised Major McCutchan not to fire. Upon further investigation it was learned that the ground forces were, indeed, U.S. troops who had captured the armored vehicles. By identifying their target closely and repeatedly seeking clarification, Major McCutchan's crew prevented a possible disaster and saved the lives of over 30 U.S. soldiers. As their award citation states, "each member of the crew displayed professional competence, aerial skill, and devotion to duty" . . . not to mention an incredible amount of discipline and discernment in the middle of a tense situation! The reservists landed after almost six hours of nerve-wracking combat time.

Meanwhile, the other half of the Reserve contingent in Panama, aircraft "Ultimate End" piloted by Captain Michael Wilson, was standing alert as a maintenance replacement aircraft for an active duty AC-130H experiencing fire control difficulties. While the active duty gunship made its time on target (TOT) over Paitilla airfield, it continued to experience problems. At 0230 hours on the morning of the 20th Captain Wilson and his crew launched on the mission to support the Navy SEAL team at Paitilla. The Reserve gunship was airborne at 0250 hours and flew a 4.4 hour close air support mission over the airfield and remained on station until it was secured by ground forces. The evening of the 20th the crew of "Ultimate End" provided close air support for elements of the 82nd Airborne in

the capture of Fort Cimmaron. As they arrived on station, the gunship crew was informed by ground forces that small arms fire was being encountered from a barracks complex. As there were two OA-37s in the area, the gunship was asked to reconnoiter the area and provide illumination passes for the jets as they made their rocket attacks on the barracks. As the OA-37s departed the scene, the gunship attacked firing its 40mm cannons. Six buildings were destroyed and numerous secondary explosions observed. Using their 20mm cannons the gunship crew also destroyed two vehicles moving in the vicinity of the friendly ground forces. As enemy opposition ceased, the ground forces asked the gunship to use its low light television to direct a medical evacuation helicopter to the landing zone and provide armed reconnaissance during the evacuation. After 8.4 hours of combat flying the crew finally returned to Howard AFB.

The Reserve personnel, both aircrew and maintenance, were all volunteers who stayed and fought after their initial commitment had expired. With only 27 deployed personnel, the 919th's support troops achieved an operational sortie rate of 100 percent while maintaining, refueling, and rearming the aircraft. The action in

Panama marked the first time reserves were engaged in combat without officially being called up.

Operation JUST CAUSE proved an ideal setting for the gunship. The fact that much of the fighting took place in and around highly populated areas only served to emphasize the Spectre's ability to provide massive, yet surgically accurate firepower. It's ability to "see" at night and distinguish friendly from enemy forces ensured mission success and no doubt saved the lives of many U.S. troops.

Gunship crews were called to action again as Operation DESERT SHIELD evolved into the shooting war of DESERT STORM. From 17 January to 27 February 1991 active duty AC-130H gunships flew 50 sorties accumulating over 280 hours.

The most successful missions proved to be preplanned interdiction missions executed according to specific battle plans. Several involved deep penetration into enemy territory to destroy early warning radar and known or suspected SCUD sites. Battle damage assessment from these missions later confirmed the destruction of several targets.

One such mission occurred on 21/22 January 1991 over Iraq as a 16th Special Operations Squadron crew hunted for SCUD sites. As they approached their target area, the

television sensor operator confirmed the target with the navigator and fire control officer. Almost immediately the gunship came under AAA fire in the form of 23mm, 37mm and 57mm fire. However, the accurate 40mm and 105mm fire laid down by the gunship destroyed two mobile missile launchers and an early warning radar facility. As the crew engaged the radar site, the electronics warfare officer received indication of an SA-8 launch and the right scanner observed an SA-14 launch. The pilots flew evasive maneuvers

reinforcements away from the area. Tragically, however, a 16th SOS AC-130H gunship, Spirit 03, was shot down in the early morning hours as it attempted to engage an Iraqi FROG (free rocket over ground) missile site threatening the U.S. Marines and Saudi National Guardsman. All 14 crew members were killed.

Along with the 1st SOW, the Reserve's 919th SOG was also deployed to Saudi Arabia. A total of 462 reserve personnel from the 919th were recalled to active duty and deployed

as the crew deployed decoy flares and the threats were defeated.

The battle for the city of Al Khafji was also significant as it was the first opportunity in DESERT STORM for the gunships to directly support ground operations. Two gunship sorties were launched on the evening of 29 January 1991 and the early morning of the 30th to support allied forces engaging Iraqis. The next evening, three missions were flown in support of coalition forces and numerous targets were destroyed. U.S. Marines involved in the battle stated that the gunships did an outstanding job in keeping Iraqi

overseas along with five AC-130A gunships and five MH-3E helicopters.

One of the most notable missions flown by 919th gunship crews occurred on the night of 26 February in support of what turned out to be "the mother of all retreats" as Iraqi soldiers attempted to leave Kuwait City for Basra. Three AC-130A crews took off from King Fahd International Airport (KFIA) on an extremely high-risk interdiction mission across heavily defended enemy lines in northern Kuwait. These were the first gunship missions conducted in enemy held territory following the shoot-down of Spirit 03 a

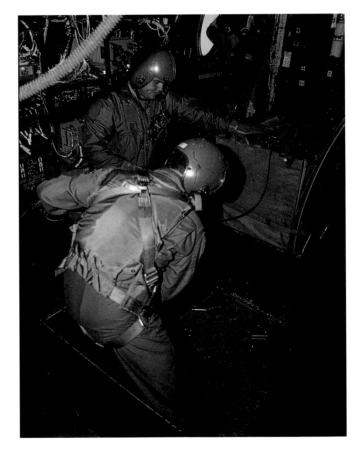

Practically every inch of space in the cargo bay of the C-130 is crowded with weapons, ammunition and sensor equipment. Along the left side of the fuselage the 20mm, 40mm and 105mm weaponry encroaches to almost the centerline of the aircraft. On the right side of the aircraft are the racks holding hundreds of rounds of ammunition plus the sensor booth housing the three sensor operators and their consoles.

Top:
Gunners load 40mm cannon set to fire at 100 rounds per minute.

Middle:
105mm can be fired as quickly as gunners can load (about 8 rounds per minute).

Bottom:
Gunners use shovels to clear empty 20mm casings. At 2500 rounds per minute the spent shells quickly pile up.

Facing Page:
As twilight approaches, smoke can be seen just below the wing tank as the 105mm howitzer is fired.

month earlier. The mission called for the crews to proceed to a holding point on the Kuwaiti border and respond quickly to any mission tasking from the airborne battlefield command and control center (ABCCC) aircraft. When tasking finally came through, the first AC-130A had already completed most of its mission time (with only 15 minutes remaining) yet the crew volunteered to attack the enemy convoys withdrawing from Kuwait City north along the Al Jahra highway. Pre-mission intelligence indicated numerous enemy threat systems still operating in the area including SA-6, SA-8, ZSU-23-4 and S-60 57mm radar guided threats as well as a variety of infrared guided missiles and heavy optical AAA. The old combat adage "when your enemy is in range . . . so are you" was no more true than on this occasion as the gunship was in the center of the enemy's threat envelope. In order to effectively employ the gunship's weapons, loitering in orbits at 10,000 feet at 160 knots, the crew was keenly aware of their vulnerability. To make matters worse, weather in the area was marginal, further reducing the probability of acquiring and engaging targets. Faced with a dwindling fuel supply, an increasing enemy threat, and deteriorating weather, the mission by most standards was clearly impractical. However, Major Michael Wilson, aircraft commander, and his co-pilot Major Clay McCutchan and the rest of the crew proceeded with the mission mindful of the risks involved.

Within minutes after receiving the call from ABCCC, they crossed the forward line of troops into enemy territory and searched for

Previous Page:
AC-130H dispenses IRCM flares.

This Page:
20mm cannons are fired for area denial affect.

Previous Page:
AC-130A, aircraft #046 "Proud Warrior" over Eglin Aux 3, Duke Field, Florida. The crew of Proud Warrior was the first gunship aircrew launched from Howard AFB during Operation JUST CAUSE and, as a result of their outstanding performance, received the Air Force Association's 1990 President's Award. JUST CAUSE was the first conflict where Air Force reservists entered direct combat without receiving a call up by a U.S. President.

This Page:
Tag Team from Hell. A 919th Special Operations Group, 711th Special Operations Squadron AC-130A working with A-10s practicing gunship escort missions. The Spectre and Warthogs are extremely compatible and both aircraft greatly compliment each others capabilities.

Following Page:
Aircraft #046 (left photo) dispensing infrared (IR) flares on Eglin ranges. The 919th SOG gunships used IR flares to defeat missile threats in both Operation JUST CAUSE and DESERT STORM.

Top Left:
Aircraft #129 "First Lady", one of the earliest prototype C-130s converted to production configuration, continues to log flight time with the 919th SOG.

Top Right:
Aircraft #014 was one of three 919th SOG AC-130As involved in the mission over Al Jahra highway on 26 January, 1991. The camels painted on the forward fuselage indicate targets destroyed.

Bottom Left:
Aircraft #509 was flown by Captain (now Major) Mike Wilson during Operation JUST CAUSE in Panama.

Bottom Right:
Aircraft #406, Proud Warrior with unpainted radar tracking dome.

Opposite Page:
Top:
Aircraft #406, Proud Warrior, with ten pineapples indicating ten targets destroyed in Panama during Operation JUST CAUSE. The TV sensor can be clearly seen in the open doorway. The access door is removed before flight.

Bottom:
Gunship nose art of "Exterminator" of the 919th SOG.

targets of opportunity in their assigned kill zone. Enroute the electronic warfare officer received several SA-8 acquisition radar warning indications which were carefully evaded. As the gunship flew eastward, numerous enemy vehicles were observed on the Jahra highway and were attacked with devastatingly accurate firepower. The crew continued northward on an erratic course for another 25 minutes until their load of 1500 rounds of 20mm and 460 rounds of 40mm ammunition was expended. With the gunship at its absolute minimum safe fuel, the crew egressed the area and headed for home at KFIA. Major Wilson's crew, having proved that the mission was feasible, though dangerous, updated the next two AC-130A gunships arriving on the scene.

Captain Richard Haddad and his crew were the second gunship to cross the border. They worked an area north of Major Wilson's flight. Early in the engagement the autopilot became inoperative and, despite the aircraft's degraded performance, the crew coordinated their efforts so well they were able to continue the mission. They destroyed at least 20 enemy trucks and four armored personnel carriers. After expending their ammunition, they too departed the area. Enroute to base the rear scanners observed three IR missiles unsuccessfully launched at their aircraft.

The third gunship, with Lt. Colonel Larry Muench's crew, crossed the border to help slow the retreating Iraqi army. On the way to their assigned kill zone, the electronic warfare officer received several SA-6 and SA-8 acquisition radar indications. All threats were evaded. As the gunship crew aquired several vehicles along the Al Jahra highway they were simultaneously locked-on by an S-60 AAA radar. Despite the threat, they continued their attack and destroyed numerous targets. Throughout the engagement,

Above:
A 919th SOG AC-130A sporting an ALQ-119 (the elongated lower pod) for decoying radar guided missiles and the bullet-shaped QRC-84-02A IR jammer pod for decoying heat seeking missiles. The gunship carries the dual pod configuration attached to a triple ejector rack (TER) mounted on the outboard pylon under each wing.

the gunship encountered small arms fire, 37mm and 57mm AAA, and received additional S-60 radar warnings. As the intensity of the threats increased and the weather worsened, the crew terminated the mission and returned safely to King Fahd. It should be noted that only hours later at least two high performance jets were shot down in the same area.

Sadly, the world does not remain a safe place for long and the gunship crews were once again called into action to support the United Nations Operations in Somalia.

On 11 June 1993 three AC-130H gunship crews participated in initial airstrikes on forces supporting Somali warlord General Mohammed Farah Aidid. Two gunships took off to work with ground forces and warned the civilian population of imminent attacks. One gunship's mission was to support the psychological operations and destroy several weapons caches in General Aidid's compound and guard house; which it accomplished with precision as several secondary explosions were observed. The crew also successfully attacked several vehicles in the immediate area. Though simple in concept, the mission was extremely complicated and required excellent coordination between navigator, FCO, and both sensor operators as cloud cover obscured the target leaving only about a third of the orbit available for attack.

To complicate matters, the other gunship was in the area simultaneously attacking "Radio Mogadishu", a Somalian radio station used by General Aidid's forces. In order to acquire its target, the second gunship had to fly overlapping orbits above the first gunship. While cloud cover hampered target identification and attack geometry, the crew pressed their attack using point-detonating and delay fused 105mm rounds. It was a masterful performance by the entire crew

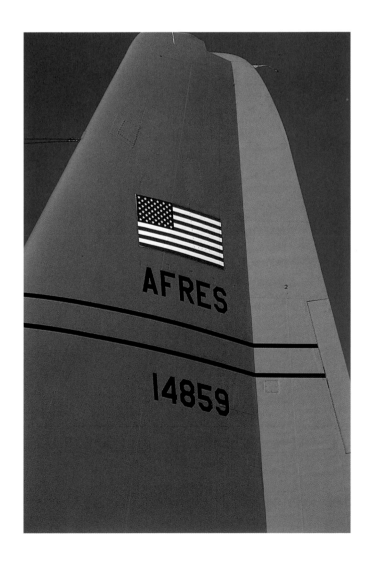

as ninety-six 105mm rounds were delivered with pinpoint accuracy.

At 20 minutes after H-hour, the third gunship commenced its attack on an armored vehicle compound. As they initiated their attack the crew experienced a multiple mission computer malfunction, forcing the gun crew to fire the 105mm using a hand-pulled lanyard. They operated in such smooth coordination that, even though the 105mm was manually fired, the gunners had the next round ready to fire as the preceding round impacted the target. In spite of the complications caused by the weather, flying through another gunship's firing orbit, and degraded gun operations, the crew still managed direct hits on several targets including the one tank in the compound.

Not every act of heroism occurs in the heat of combat. On 16 June 1993, an AC-130H taking off from Mogadishu on a mission in support of ground forces experienced an engine fire 100 feet above the ground. Fully loaded with fuel and ammunition, the crew had to act quickly to save the airplane. Due to the professional competence, aerial skill and disciplined crew coordination, the aircraft was able to return to base – though just barely as the crew performed a two-engine, no-flap landing with a 15 knot tailwind.

As gunship crews continue to perfect their close air support techniques and as modifications and new technologies improve the gunship's capabilities, potential enemies will learn the hard way that the Spectre is not a ghost or an apparition – but a deadly reality of modern combat.

Below:
Flightline engine maintenance on a 711th SOS AC-130A.

Facing Page:
(Top) The Duke Field Magic. Maintenance technicians of the 919th SOG have received numerous Air Force awards for their outstanding work. The 919th's AC-130A's are the oldest flying combat aircraft in the U.S. Air Force inventory.

Bottom:
919th SOG gunners loading 40mm ammunition during a firing pass. Manning the cannons is an extremely physical and demanding job with the aircraft jostling in the turbulence at 5,000 feet, banking at 30 degrees and pulling between 1.5 and 2 g's during turns.

ACKNOWLEDGMENTS

The AIR COMMANDOS book project has been a group effort from the start.

Major General Bruce Fister graciously provided the all important go ahead.

Shirley Sikes and Captain Kim Urie spent untold hours working and following up on my varied requests. They provided escort in all sorts of weather and, on more than one occasion, endured grueling late night flights. I am in awe of their professionalism . . . and especially thankful for their friendship.

JoAnna Couch and Major Dave Mason did their best to convert my ramblings into something intelligible and printable.

Mike Faulkner offered encouragement when the idea for the book was but a gleam in the author's eye.

Lt. Colonel Clay McCutchan, Major Janet Tucker, CMSgt. Michael Hosenbackez, Sgt. Tim Hadrych and Sgt. Randy Bergeron shared their knowledge, experiences and keen insight.

Colonel Walter Ernst, Lt. Colonel Mike Homan, Lt. Colonel Rod Reay, Lt. Colonel John Zarht, Major Paul Harmon, Major Jeff Urie and Captain Brenda Campbell made things happen so that AFSOC activities could be seen and photographed in daylight . No small task for a Command that owns the night. I cannot thank them enough for their above and beyond the call of duty efforts.

And to all the maintenance, life support and flight crews who endured my clumsiness and awkwardness with flight gear, safety harnesses, and what would appear to be the simple act of getting into and out of an aircraft – my heartfelt thanks!

Finally, for her patience and long suffering, I thank my sweet wife Andrea.